Imperial Japane   WW 2.

Compiled By:- J Atkinson.

The information contained in the following pages has been compiled by
John Atkinson with the aid of

The Gosport Library (Reference Section)

Various other sources

Published by Galago Books
42 Palace Grove
Bromley
Kent BR1 3HB
England

First printing 2002
ISBN 0-946995-73-7

Photographs:
Front Cover – *Battleship Ashigara*
Back Cover Top: - *Battleship Nagato*
Back Cover Bottom – *Battleship Yamato*

JAPANESE WARSHIP LOSSES.

BATTLESHIPS.

Yamato Class.
Displacement: 69,990 Tonnes.   **Complement:** 2,500.
Dimensions: 839'11" x 121'1" x 34'1".
Machinery: 12 Boilers, 4 Shaft geared turbines. 150,000 Shp = 27Kts.
Fuel Cap: 6,300 Tons. Range: Unknown.
Armament: 9 x 18.1", 12 x 6.1", 12 x 5", 24" 3 x 3", 6 x 2", 4 x 0.3",
     24 x 25mm AA, 4 x 13.2mm AA.
Armour: Belt 16.1", Deck 9.1" Max, 21.5", Turrets 25.6" Max,
     Conning Tower 19.7" Max.
Aircraft: 7.

Name.	Builder.	Laid dwn.	Launched.	Completed.
YAMATO.	Kure Navy yd.	04-11-37.	08-08-40.	16-12-41.

Fate: Sunk. 07-04-45. 13 Torpedoes + 6 bombs Whilst approaching Okinawa.

Name.	Builder.	Laid dwn.	Launched.	Completed.
MUSHASI.	Mitsubishi, Nagasaki.	23-03-38.	01-11-40.	05-08-42.

Fate: Sunk. 24-10-44. By US Navy A/c 19 Torpedoes + 17 Bombs, Battle of the Sibuyan Sea.

Name.	Builder.	Laid dwn.	Launched.	Completed.
SHINANO.	Yokosuka Navy yd.	04-05-40.	08-10-44.	19-11-44.

Fate: Converted to aircraft carrier 1942-44 (See aircraft carriers).

FUSO Class.
Displacement: 38,000 Tonnes.   **Complement:** 1,396.
Dimensions: 698'0" x 100'6" x 31'9".
Machinery: 6 Boilers, 4 Shaft geared turbines. 75,000 Shp = 24.7Kts.
Fuel Cap: 5,100 Tons. Range: Unknown.
Armament: 12 x 14", 14 x 6", 8 x 5", 16 x 25mm AA, 3 A/c.
Armour: Deck 3.8-7" Max..
Aircraft: 7.

Name.	Builder.	Laid dwn.	Launched.	Completed.
FUSO.	Kure Navy yd.	11-03-12.	28-03-14.	08-11-15.

Fate: Sunk. 25-10-44. 2 Torpedoes from US Destroyers.

Name.	Builder.	Laid dwn.	Launched.	Completed.
YAMASHIRO.	Yokosuka Navy yd.	20-11-13.	03-11-15.	31-03-17.

Fate: Sunk. Date unknown. 4 Torpedoes from US Destroyers.

BATTLESHIPS. (Continued).

ISE Class.
Displacement: 39,535 Tonnes.   Complement: 1,376.
Dimensions: 708'0" x 140'0" x 30'2".
Machinery: 8 Boilers, 4 Shaft geared turbines. 00,000 Shp = 25.3Kts.
Fuel Cap: 5,313 Tons. Range: Unknown.
Armament: 12 x 14", 16 x 5.5", 8 x 5", 20 x 25mm AA, 3 A/c.
Armour: Deck 3.8-7" Max.
Aircraft: 7.

Name.	Builder.	Laid dwn.	Launched.	Completed.
ISE.	Kawasaki Kobe.	10-05-15.	12-11-16.	15-12-17.

Fate: Sunk. Battle of Surigao Strait.

Name.	Builder.	Laid dwn.	Launched.	Completed.
HYUGA.	Mitsibushi Nagasaki.	06-05-15.	21-01-16.	30-04-17.

Fate: Sunk. Battle of Surigao Strait.

NAGATO Class.
Displacement: 39,120 Tonnes.   Complement: 1368.
Dimensions: 738'0" x 108'2" x 31'2".
Machinery: 10 Boilers, 4 Shaft geared turbines. 82,000 Shp = 25Kts.
Fuel Cap: Unknown. Range: Unknown.
Armament: 8 x 16", 18 x 5.5", 8 x 5", 20 x 25mm AA, 3 A/c.
Armour: Belt 11.8" Max, Deck 3.5-7" Max, Turrets 14", Conning Tower 12".
Aircraft: 3.

Name.	Builder.	Laid dwn.	Launched.	Completed.
NAGATO.	Kure Navy yd.	28-08-17.	09-11-19.	25-11-20.

Fate: 29-07-46. Expended as target in Bikini Attol 'A' Bomb tests.

Name.	Builder.	Laid dwn.	Launched.	Completed.
MUTSU.	Yokosuka Navy yd.	01-06-17.	31-05-20.	24-10-20.

Fate: Lost. 08-06-43. Internal explosion in the Inland Sea.

AIRCRAFT CARRIERS.

HOSHO (Class).

Displacement:	10,000 Tonnes. Complement: 550.
Dimensions:	817'0" x 103'0" x 28'6".
Machinery:	12 Boilers, 2 Shaft geared turbines. 30,000Shp = 31.5Kts.
Fuel Cap:	(Oil) 2695 tons, (Coal) 940 Tons. Range: 8,000Nm @ 15 Kts.
Armour:	Unknown.
Armament:	4 x 5.5", 2 x 3.0"AA, 2 MG, 26 Aircraft.

Name.	Builder.	Laid dwn.	Launched.	Completed.
HOSHO.	Asano, Tsurumi.	16-12-19.	13-11-21.	16-12-22.

Fate: Scrapped after being used as a repatriation transport.

AKAGI (Class).

Displacement:	42,750 Tonnes. Complement: 2,000.
Dimensions:	855'2" x 102'9" x 28'7"
Machinery:	19 Boilers, 4 Shaft geared turbines. 131,200Shp = 32.5 Kts.
Fuel Cap:	(Oil) 6,000 Tons, Range: 8,000Nm @ 14 Kts.
Armour:	Belt 10".
Armament:	10 x 8", 12 x 4.7"AA, 14 x 25mm AA, 91 A/c.

Name.	Builder.	Laid dwn.	Launched.	Completed.
AKAGI.	Kure, Navy yd.	06-12-20.	22-04-25.	25-03-27.

Fate: Sunk. 05-06-42. By US Navy A/c in the Battle of Midway.

KAGA Class.

Displacment:	43,650 Tonnes. Complement: 13,40.
Dimensions:	782'6" x 97'0" x 26'0".
Machinery:	12 Boilers, 4 Shaft geared turbines. 127,500Shp = 28.34Kts.
Fuel Cap:	(Oil) 7,500 Tons. Range: Unknown.
Armour:	Belt. 11.0".
Armament:	16 x 5", 12 x 4.7", 22 x 25mm AA, 72 Aircraft.

Name.	Builder.	Laid dwn.	Launched.	Completed.
KAGA.	Kawasaki, Kobe.	19-07-20.	17-11-21.	31-03-28.

Fate: Sunk. 04-06-42. By US Navy A/c, Aircraft fuel tanks explosion in the Battle of Midway.

AIRCRAFT CARRIERS. (Continued).

RYUJO (Class).

Displacement: 13,650 Tonnes.   Complement: 600.

Dimensions:	513'6" x 75'2" x 18'3".
Machinery;	6 Boilers, 2 Shaft geared turbines. 66,000Shp 29Kts.
Fuel Cap:	(Oil) 2,490 Tons. Range: 10,000 Nm @ 14Kts.
Armour:	Light plating, Machinery spaces/Magazines
Armament:	12 x 5.0", 22 x 25mm AA, 24 x 13mm AA, 37 Aircraft.

Name.	Builder.	Laid dwn.	Launched.	Completed.
RYUJO.	Yokohama Co.	26-11-29.	02-04-31.	09-03-33.

Sunk: 24-08-42. by 4 bombs + 1 torpedo, Battle for the eastern Solomons.

SORYU (Class).

Displacement: 19,800 Tonnes.   Complement: 11,000.

Dimensions:	746'6" x 69'11" x 25'0".
Machinery:	8 Boilers, 4 Shaft geared turbines. 153,000Shp = 34.5Kts.
Fuel Cap:	(Oil) 44,000 Tons. Range: Unknown.
Armour:	Belt. 1.8", Machinery spaces/Magazines 5.9", Deck. 1.0".
Armament:	12 x 5.0", 28 x 25mm AA, 71 Aircraft.

Name.	Builder.	Laid dwn.	Launched.	Completed.
SORYU.	Kure Navy yd.	20-11-34.	23-12-35.	29-12-37.

Fate: Sunk. 04-06-42. By US Navy A/c 3 bombs in the Battle of Midway.

HIRYU (Class).

Displacement: 21,900 Tonnes.   Complement: 1,101.

Dimensions:	745'11" x 88'6" x 25'9".
Machinery:	8 Boilers, 4 Shaft geared turbines. 153,000Shp + 34.3Kts.
Range:	Unknown. Range: Unknown.
Fuel Cap:	(Oil) 4,400 Tons.
Armour:	Belt. 3.5", Machinery Spaces/Magazines 5.9", Deck. 1.0".
Armament:	12 x 5.0", 31 x 25mm AA, 64 Aircraft.

Name.	Builder.	Laid dwn.	Launched.	Completed.
HIRYU.	Yokosuka Navy yd.	08-07-36.	16-11-37.	05-07-39.

Fate: Sunk. 05-06-42. By US Navy A/c 4 bombs in the Battle of Midway.

AIRCRAFT CARRIERS. (Continued).

SHOKAKU (Class).

Displacement: 32,619. Tonnes.   Complement: 1,660.
Dimensions: 844'10" x 85'4" x 29'1".
Machinery: 8 Boilers, 4 Shaft geared turbines. 160'000Shp = 34.2Kts.
Fuel Cap: (Oil) 5,385 Tons. Range: 10'000Nm @ 18Kts.
Armour: Belt. 1.8", Magazines. 6.5", Deck. 3.9".
Armament: 16 x 5.0", 42 x 25mm AA, 72 A/c.

Name.	Builder.	Laid dwn.	Launched.	Completed.
SHOKAKU.	Yokosuka Navy yd.	12-12-37.	01-06-39.	08-08-41.

Fate: Sunk. 19-06-44. By US S/m CAVALLA. 3 Torpedoes in the Battle of the Phillipines.

Name.	Builder.	Laid dwn.	Launched.	Completed.
ZUIKAKU.	Kawasaki Kobe.	25-05-38.	27-11-39.	25-09-41.

Fate: Sunk. 25-10-44. By US Navy A/c 6 Torpedoes & 7 Bombs in the Battle of Cape Engano.

ZUIHO (Class).

Displacement: 14'200 Tonnes.   Complement: 785.
Dimensions: 671'11" x 59'9" x 21'9".
Machinery: 4 Boilers, 2 Shaft geared turbines. 52'000Shp =28Kts.
Fuel Cap: (Oil) 2'600 Tons. Range Unknown.
Armament: 8 x 5.0", 8 x 25mm AA, 6 x 8 Barreled rockets. 30 Aircraft.

Name.	Builder.	Laid dwn.	Launched.	Completed.
ZUIHO.	Yokosuka Navy yd.	20-06-35.	19-06-36.	27-12-40.

Fate: Sunk. 25-10-44. By US Navy A/c Bombs + Torpedoes in the Battle of the Coral Sea.

Name.	Builder.	Laid dwn.	Launched.	Completed.
SHOHO.	Yokosukan Navy yd.	03-12-34.	01-06-35.	27-12-40.

Fate: Sunk. 07-05-42. By US Navy A/c 11 Bombs + 7 Torpedoes in the Battle of the Coral Sea.

RYUHO (Class).

Displacement: 15,060 Tonnes.   Complement: 989.
Dimensions: 650'0" x 75'6" x 21'10".
Machinery: 4 Boilers, 2 Shaft geared turbines. 52,000Shp = 26.5Kts.
Fuel Cap: (Oil) 2'900Tons. Range: 8,000Nm @ 18Kts.
Armour: Deck. 0.4".
Armament: 8 x 5.0", 61 x 25mm AA, 6 x 28 Barrelled rockets, 31 Aircraft.

Name.	Builder.	Laid dwn.	Launched.	Completed.
RYUHO.	Yokosuka Navy yd.	12-04-33.	16-11-33.	28-11-42.

Fate: 17-03-45. Serious damage during air-raid at Kure docks, Scrapped after surrender.

AIRCRAFT CARRIERS. (Continued).

JUNYO (Class).

Displacement: 28,300 Tonnes.   Complement: 1,224.
Dimensions: 719'6" x 87'7" x 26'9".
Machinery: 6 Boilers, 2 Shaft geared turbines, 56,250Shp.
Fuel Cap: (Oil). 2'800 Tons. Range: Unknown.
Armour: Unknown.
Armament: 12 x 5.0", 24 x 25mm AA, 53 A/c.

Name.	Builder.	Laid dwn.	Launched.	Completed.
JUNYO.	Mitsubishi Nagasaki.	20-03-39.	26-06-41.	05-05-42.

Fate: Broken up 1947.

Name.	Builder.	Laid dwn.	Launched.	Completed.
HIYO.	Kawasaki Kobe.	30-11-39.	24-06-41.	31-07-42.

Fate: Sunk. 20-06-44. By US Navy A/c in the Battle of the Phillipine Sea.

TAIHO (Class).

Displacement: 37,720 Tonnes.   Compliment: 1,751.
Dimensions: 855'0" x 90'11" x 31'6".
Machinery: 8 Boilers, 4 Shaft geared turbines. 160,000Shp = 33.3Kts.
Fuel Cap: (Oil) 5,700 Tons. Unknown.
Armour: Machinery 2.2", Magazine's 5.9", Flight Deck 3.1", Lower Hangar 4.9".
Armament: 12 x 3.9" AA, 51 x 25mm AA, 53 A/c.

Name.	Builder.	Laid dwn.	Launched.	Completed.
TAIHO.	Kawasaki Kobe.	10-07-41.	07-04-43.	07-03-44.

Fate: Sunk. 19-06-44. 1 Torpedo causing internal explosion.

CHITOSE (Class).

Displacement: 15,300 Tonnes.   Complement: 800.
Dimensions: 631'7" x 68'3" x 24'8".
Machinery: 4 Boilers, 2 Shaft geared turbines. 44,000Shp = 28.9Kts.
                           Diesel Motors. 12,800Bhp = 28.9Kts.
Fuel Cap: (Oil). 3,000 Tons. Range: Unknown.
Armour: Unknown.
Armament: 8 x 5", 30 x 25mm, 24 A/c.

Name.	Builder.	Laid dwn.	Launched.	Completed.
CHITOISE.	Kure Navy yd.	26-11-34.	29-11-36.	01-01-44.

Fate: Sunk. 25-10-44. Bomb damage, Battle of Cape Engano.

Name.	Builder.	Laid dwn.	Launched.	Completed.
CHYODA.	Kure Navy yd.	14-12-36.	19-11-37.	31-10-43.

Fate: Sunk. Bomb damage, Battle of Cape Engano..

AIRCRAFT CARRIERS. (Continued).

SHINANO (Class). *(Ex YAMATO Class Battleship).*
Displacement: 65,837 Tonnes.   **Complement:** 2,400.
Dimensions: 872'8" x 119'1" x 33'10".
Machinery: 12 Boilers. 4 Shaft geared turbines. 150,000Shp = 27Kts.
Fuel Cap: (Oil). 8,900 Tons. Range: 10,000Nm @ 18Kts..
Armour: Belt 8.1", Flight Deck 3.1", Hanger deck 7.5".
Armament: 16 x 5", 145 x 25mm AA, 12 x 28 Barreled rockets, 120 Aircraft.

Name.	Builder.	Laid dwn.	Launched.	Completed.
SHINANO.	Yokosuka Navy yd.	04-05-40.	08-10-44.	19-11-44.

Fate: Sunk. 19-12-44. 4 Torpedoes from US S/m ARCHERFISH.

UNRYU (Class).
Displacement: 22,860 Tonnes.   **Complement:** 1,595.
Dimensions: 746'1" x 72'2" x 25'9".
Machinery: 8 Boilers, 4 Shaft geared turbines. 152,000Shp =34Kts.
Fuel Cap: (Oil). 3,670 Tons. Range: Unknown.
Armour: Belt. 1.8", Magazines. 5.9", Deck. 1.0".
Armament: 12 x 5.0", 89 x 25mm AA, 6 x 8 Barrelled rockets, 65 x A/c.

Name.	Builder.	Laid dwn.	Launched.	Completed.
UNRYU.	Yokosuka Navy yd.	01-08-42.	25-09-43.	06-08-44.

Fate: Sunk. 24-07-45. 2 Torpedoes from US>S/m. REDFISH.

Name.	Builder.	Laid dwn.	Launched.	Completed.
AMAGI.	Mitsibushi ,Nagasaki.	01-10-42.	15-10-43.	10-08-44.

Fate: Sunk. By US Navy A/c in shallow water at Kure.

Name.	Builder.	Laid dwn.	Launched.	Completed.
KATSURAGI.	Kure Navy yd.	08-12-42.	19-01-44.	15-10-44.

Fate: Broken up, after repatriation duties.

Name.	Builder.	Laid dwn.	Launched.	Completed.
KASAGI.	Kure Navy yd.	No further information.		

Fate: Broken up 1947.

Name.	Builder.	Laid dwn.	Launched.	Completed.
IKOMA.	Kure Navy yd.	No further information.		

Fate: Broken up 1947.

AIRCRAFT CARRIERS. (Continued).

IBUKI (Class).

Displacement: 14,570 Tonnes.   Complement: 1,015.
Dimensions: 672'7" x 69'9" x 20'8".
Machinery·   4 Boilers, 2 Shaft geared turbines. 72'0003hp – 29Kts.
Fuel Cap: Unknown. Range: Unknown.
Armour: Unknown.
Armament: 4 x 3.0" AA, 48 x 25mm AA, 24 Aircraft.

Name.	Builder.	Laid dwn.	Launched.	Completed.
IBUKI.	Kure Navy yd.	24-04-42.	21-05-43.	Uncompleted.

Fate: Broken up 1947.

KAIYO (Class). Escort Carrier.

Displacement: 16,483 Tonnes.   Complement: 829.
Dimensions: 546'5" x 71'10" x 26'5".
Machinery: 4 Boilers, 2 Shaft geared turbines. 52,000Shp = 24Kts.
Fuel Cap: Unknown. Range: Unknown.
Armour: Unknown.
Armament: 8 x 5.0", 24 x 25mm AA, 24 Aircraft.

Name.	Builder.	Laid dwn.	Launched.	Completed.
KAIYO.	Mitsibushi Nagasaki.	Unknown.	09-12-38.	23-11-43.

Fate: Broken up 1947.

TAIYO Class. Escort Carrier.

Displacement: 19,700 Tonnes.   Complement: Taiyo 747. Unyo/Chuyo 850.
Dimensions: 591'4" x 73'10" x 26'3".
Machinery: 4 Boilers, 2 Shaft geared turbines. 25,200Shp = 21Kts.
Fuel Cap: Unknown. Range: 6,500Nm @ 18Kts.
Armour: Unknown.
Armament: Taiyo 6 x 4.7", Unyo/Chuyo 8 x 5.0" AA, 8 x 25mm AA.

Name.	Builder.	Laid dwn.	Launched.	Completed.
TAIYO.	Mitsibushi, Nagasaki.	Unknown.	19-09-40.	15-09-41.

Fate: Sunk. 18-08-44. Torpedoed by US.S/m RASHER.

Name.	Builder.	Laid dwn.	Launched.	Completed.
UNYO.	Mitsibushi, Nagasaki.	Unknown.	31-10-39.	31-05-42.

Fate: Sunk, 16-09-44. Torpedoed by US.S/m BARB.

Name.	Builder.	Laid dwn.	Launched.	Completed.
CHUYO.	Misibushi, Nagasaki.	Unknown.	20-05-39.	25-11-42.

Fate: Torpedoed by US.S/m SAILFISH.

AIRCRAFT CARRIERS. (Continued).

SHINYO (Class).

Displacement: 20,586 Tonnes.   Complement: 942.
Dimensions: 621'3" x 84'0" x 26'10".
Machinery: 4 Boilers, 2 Shaft geared turbines, 26,000Shp = 22Kts.
Fuel Cap: Unknown. Range: Unknown.
Armour: Unknown.
Armament: 8 x 5.0", 42 x 25mm AA, 33 Aircraft.

Name.	Builder.	Laid dwn.	Launched.	Completed.
SHINYO.	Deschimag, Bremen.	Unknown.	14-12-34.	15-12-43.

Fate: Sunk. 17-11-44. Torpedoed in the Yellow Sea by US.S/m SPADEFISH.

CRUISERS.

KONGO (Class).
Displacement: 36,000 Tonnes. (Max).   Complement: 1,437.
Dimensions: 738'7" x 95'3" x 31'11".
Machinery: 8 Boilers, 3 Shaft geared turbines. 57,000Shp = 33.3Kts.
Fuel Cap: (Oil). 830 Tons. Range: Unknown.
Armour: Belt. 2.3", Deck. 1.0", Gun houses. 1.0".
Armament: 6 x 5.5", 1 x 3.0" AA, 2 MG, 4 x 24"TT, Mines 34.

Name.	Builder.	Laid dwn.	Launched.	Completed.
KONGO.	Vickers (GB).	17-01-11.	Unknown.	16-08-13.

Fate: Sunk. 21-11-44. Torpedoed by US S/m SEALION.

Name.	Builder.	Laid dwn.	Launched.	Completed.
HIEI.	Mitsibushi Yokosuka.	04-11-11	21-11-12.	04-08-14.

Fate: Sunk. 1st Battle of Guadacanal. Finished off by Arial Torpedoes.

Name.	Builder.	Laid dwn.	Launched.	Completed.
KIRISHIMA.	Mitsibushi Yokosuka.	17-03-12.	01-12-13.	19-04-15.

Fate: Scuttled. 15-11-42. 2nd Battle of Guadacanal.

Name.	Builder.	Laid dwn.	Launched.	Completed.
HARUNA.	Kawasaki Kobe.	16-03-12.	14-12-13.	19-04-15.

Fate: Sunk. 28-07-45. By US A/c near Kure.

SENDAI. (Class).
Displacement: 5,195 Tonnes.   Complement: 450.
Dimensions: 535'0" x 46'9" x 15'11".
Machinery: 12 Boilers, 4 Shaft geared turbines. 70,000Shp = 33Kts.
Fuel Cap: (Oil). 1,200 Tons. Range: Unknown.
Armour: Belt. 2", Deck. 2".
Armament: 7 x 5.5", 2 x 3.0" AA, 6 MG, 6 x 21"TT, A/c 3.

Name.	Builder.	Laid dwn.	Launched.	Completed.
SENDAI.	Mitsibushi Nagasaki.	16-02-22.	30-10-23.	29-04-24.

Fate: Sunk. 02-11-43. After heavy damage, during the Battle of Empress Augusta Bay.
Finally sunk by carrier A/c.

Name.	Builder.	Laid dwn.	Launched.	Completed.
NAKA.	Mitsibushi Yokohama.	10-06-22.	24-03-25.	30-11-25.

Fate: Sunk. 17-02-44. By US carrier A/c. Off Truk in the Carolines.

Name.	Builder.	Laid dwn.	Launched.	Completed.
JINTSU.	Kawasaki Kobe.	04-08-22.	08-12-23.	31-07-25.

Fate: Sunk. 13-07-43. Gunfire and Torpedoes. At the Battle of Kolombangara

CRUISERS. (Continued).

YUBARI (Class).
Displacement: 3,141 Tonnes.   Complement: 328.
Dimensions: 455'0" x 39'6" x 11'9".
Machinery: 8 Boilers, 3 Shaft geared turbines. 57,000Shp = 35.5Kts.
Fuel Cap: (Oil). 830 Tons. Range: Unknown.
Armour: Belt. 2.3", Deck. 1.0", Gun houses. 1.0".
Armament: 6 x 5.5", 1 x 3.0" AA, 2 MG, 4 x 24"TT, Mines 34.

Name.	Builder.	Laid dwn.	Launched.	Completed.
YUBARI.	Sasebo Navy yd.	05-06-22.	05-03-23.	31-07-23.

Fate: Sunk. Torpedoed by US.S/m BLUEGILL.

FORUTAKA (Class).
Displacement: 8,450 Tonnes.   Complement: 625.
Dimensions: 607'6" x 51'9" x 18'3".
Machinery: 12 Boilers, 4 Shaft geared turbines. 102,000Shp = 34.5Kts.
Fuel Cap: (Oil). 1,400 Tons. Range: Unknown.
Armour: Belt. 3.0", Deck. 1.4", Gun houses. 1.0".
Armament: 6 x 8.0", 4 x 3.0" AA, 2 MG, 12 x 24"TT, Mines None, 1 A/c.

Name.	Builder.	Laid dwn.	Launched.	Completed.
FURUTAKA.	Mitsibushi Nagasaki.	05-12-22.	25-02-25.	31-03-26.

Fate: Sunk. 11-10-42. Gunfire & Torpedoes at the Battle of Cape Esperance.

Name.	Builder.	Laid dwn.	Launched.	Completed.
KAKO.	Kawasaki Kobe.	17-11-22.	10-04-25.	20-07-26.

Fate: Sunk. 10-08-42. Torpedoed by US. S/m S44.

AOBA (Class).
Displacement: 8,760 Tonnes.   Complement: 625.
Dimensions: 607'6" x 51'11" x 18'9".
Machinery: 12 Boilers, 4 Shaft geared turbines. 102,000Shp = 34.5Kts.
Fuel Cap: (Oil) 1.800 Tons. Range: Unknown.
Armour: Belt.3.0", Deck. 1.4", Gun houses. 1.0".
Armament: 6 x 8.0", 4 x 4.7" AA, 2 MG, 12 x 24"TT, 1 A/c.

Name.	Builder.	Laid dwn.	Launched.	Completed.
AOBA.	Mitsibushi Nagasaki.	04-02-24.	25-09-26.	20-09-27.

Fate: Sunk. 28-07-45. US A/c at Kobe in shallow water. Scrapped 1948.

Name.	Builder.	Laid dwn.	Launched.	Completed.
KINUGASA.	Kawasaki Kobe.	23-01-24.	24-10-26.	30-09-27.

Fate: Sunk. 14-11-42. By US Navy A/c in the Battle of Guadalcanal.

CRUISERS. (Continued).

NACHI (Class).

Displacement: 13,120 Tonnes.		Complement: 773.
Dimensions:	668'6" x 56'11" x 19'4".	
Machinery:	12 Boilers, 4 Shaft geared turbines. 130,000Shp = 35.5Kts.	
Fuel Cap:	(Oil) 2,470 Tons. Range: Unknown.	
Armour:	Belt 3.9", Deck. 1.4", Turrets. 1.0".	
Armament:	10 x 8.0", 6 x 4.7" AA, 2 MG, 12 x 24"TT, 2 Aircraft.	

Name.	Builder.	Laid dwn.	Launched.	Completed.
NACHI.	Kure Navy yd.	26-11-24.	15-06-27.	26-11-28.

Fate: Sunk. 05-11-44. US Navy A/c in Manila Bay.

Name.	Builder.	Laid dwn.	Launched.	Completed.
MYOKO.	Yokosuka Navy yd.	25-10-24.	16-04-27.	31-07-29.

Fate: Scuttled. 08-07-45. Torpedoed by US. S/m BERGAIL during the Battle of Leyte Gulf.

Name.	Builder.	Laid dwn.	Launched.	Completed.
HAGURO.	Mitsibushi Nagasaki.	16-03-25.	24-03-28.	25-04-29.

Fate: Sunk. 16-05-45. 8 Torpedoes from British destroyers, off Penang.

Name.	Builder.	Laid dwn.	Launched.	Completed.
ASHIGARA.	Kawasaki Kobe.	11=04-25.	22-04-28.	20-08-29.

Fate: Sunk. 08-06-45. 5 torpedoes from HMS/m. TRENCHANT. Near Banka Strait.

TAKAO (Class).

Displacement: 12,781 Tonnes.		Compliment: 773.
Dimensions:	668'6" x 59'2" x 20'1".	
Machinery:	12 Boilers, 4 Shaft geared turbines. 130,000Shp = 35.5Kts.	
Fuel Cap:	(Oil). 2,570 Tons. Range: Unknown.	
Armour:	Belt. 3.9", Magazines. 4.9", Deck. 1.4", Turrets. 1.0".	
Armament:	10 x 8", 4 x 4.7" AA, 2 x 40mm AA, 8 x 24"TT, A/c. 3.	

Name.	Builder.	Laid dwn.	Launched.	Completed.
TAKAO.	Yokosuka. Navy yd.	28-04-27.	12-05-30.	31-05-32.

Fate: Sunk. 31-07-45. Singapore. by HMS/m XE3 side cargoes.
Finally scuttled Malacca Straits 27-10-46.

Name.	Builder.	Laid dwn.	Launched.	Completed.
ATAGO.	Kure Navy yd.	28-04-27.	16-06-30.	30-03-32.

Fate: Sunk. 23-10-44. 4 Torpedoes from US.S/m DARTER. Battle of Leyte Gulf.

Name.	Builder.	Laid dwn.	Launched.	Completed.
MAYA.	Kawasaki Kobe.	04-12-28	08-11-30.	30-06-32.

Fate: Sunk. 23-10-44. 4 Torpedoes from US.S/m DACE. Battle of Leyte Gulf.

Name.	Builder.	Laid dwn.	Launched.	Completed.
CHOKAI.	Mitsibushi Nagasaki.	26-03-28.	05-04-31.	30-06-32.

Fate: Sunk. (Date Unknown). US Navy A/c in the Battle of Samar.

CRUISERS. (Continued).

MOGAMI (Class).
Displacement: 10,993 Tonnes.   Complement: 850.
Dimensions: 661'1" x 59'1" x 18'1".
Machinery: 10 Boilers, 4 Shaft geared turbines. 150,000Shp = 37Kts.
Fuel Cap: (Oil). 2,163 Tons. Range: Unknown.
Armour: Belt. 3.9". Magazines. 4.9". Deck. 1.4"- 2.4". Turrets. 1.0".
Armament: 15 x 6.1", 8 x 5.0", 4 x 40mm AA, 12 x 24"TT, A/c 3.

Name.	Builder.	Laid dwn.	Launched.	Completed.
MOGAMI.	Kure Navy yd.	27-10-31.	14-03-34.	28-07-35.

Fate: Sunk. 25-10-44. Serious damage by US Navy A/c in the Battle of Surigo Strait. Finally torpedoed by A/c.

Name.	Builder.	Laid dwn.	Launched.	Completed.
MIKUMA.	Mitsibushi Nagasaki.	24-12-31.	31-05-34.	28-07-35.

Fate: Sunk. 06-06-42. By US Navy A/c in the Battle of Midway.

Name.	Builder.	Laid dwn.	Launched.	Completed.
SUZAYA.	Yokosuko Navy yd.	11-12-33.	20-11-31.	31-10-37.

Fate: Sunk. 25-10-44. By US Navy A/c in the Battle of Saymar.

Name.	Builder.	Laid dwn.	Launched.	Completed.
Kumano.	Kawasaki Kobe.	05-04-34.	15-10-36.	31-10-37.

Fate: Sunk.25-11-44. Bombed in Dasol Bay (Phillipines).

TONE (Class).
Displacement: 15,200 Tonnes.   Complement: 850.
Dimensions: 661'0" x 60'8" x 21'3".
Machinery: 8 Boilers, 4 Shaft geared turbines. 152,000Shp = 35Kts.
Fuel Cap: (Oil). Range: Unknown.
Armour: Belt. 3.9". Magazines. 4.9". Deck. 1.2". Turrets. 1.0".
Armment: 8 x 8.0", 8 x 5.0", 12 x 25mm AA, 12 x 24"TT.

Name.	Builder.	Laid dwn.	Launched.	Completed.
TONE.	Mitsibushi Nagasaki.	01-12-34.	21-11-37.	20-11-38.

Fate: Sunk. 24-07-45. Bombed in shallow water near Kure. Scrapped 1948.

Name.	Builder.	Laid dwn.	Launched.	Completed.
CHIKUMA.	Mitsibushi Nagasaki.	01-10-35.	19-03-38.	20-05-39.

Fate: Sunk. Bombed & Torpedoed by US Navy A/c during the Battle of Samar.

CRUISERS. (Continued).

KATORI (Class).
Displacement: 6,180 Tonnes.   Complement: Unknown.
Dimensions: 452'9" x 52'4" x 18'10".
Machinery: 3 Boilers, 2 Shaft geared turbines + Diesel motors. 8,000Shp = 18Kts.
Fuel Cap: Unknown. Range: Unknown.
Armour: Deck. 2.0".
Armament: 4 x 5.5", 2 x 5.0", 4 x 25mm AA, 4 x 21"TT, A/c x 1.

Name.	Builder.	Laid dwn.	Launched.	Completed.
KATORI.	Mitsibushi Yokohama.	24-08-38.	17-06-39.	20-04-44.

Fate: Sunk. 17-02-44. By gunfire, near Truk.

Name.	Builder.	Laid dwn.	Launched.	Completed.
KASHII.	As above.	30-05-40.	14-02-41.	05-12-41.

Fate: Sunk. 12-01-45. By US Navy A/c.

Name.	Builder.	Laid dwn.	Launched.	Completed.
KASIMA.	Broken up 1947. No other information available.			

Name.	Builder.	Laid dwn.	Launched.	Completed.
KASHIWARA.	Broken up 1947. No other information available.			

AGANO (Class).
Displacement: 8,534 Tonnes.   Complement: 730.
Dimensions: 571'2" x 49'10" x 18'6".
Machinery: 6 Boilers. 4 Shaft geared turbines. 100,000Shp = 35Kts.
Fuel Cap: (Oil). 405 Tons. Range: Unknown.
Armour: Belt. 2.2", Magazines 2.0", Deck 0.7", Turrets 1.0".
Armament: 6 x 6.0", 4 x 3.0" AA, 32 x 25mm AA, 8 x 24"TT, 16 DC, A/c x 2.

Name.	Builder.	Laid dwn.	Launched.	Completed.
AGANO.	Sasebo Navy yd.	18-06-40.	22-10-41.	31-10-42.

Fate: Sunk. 17-02-44. Torpedoed by US.S/m SKATE.

Name.	Builder.	Laid dwn.	Launched.	Completed.
NOSHIRO.	Yokosuka Navy yd.	04-09-41.	19-07-42.	30-06-43.

Fate: Sunk. 26-10-44. Bombed by US Navy A/c in the Retreat from the Battle of Samar.

Name.	Builder.	Laid dwn.	Launched.	Completed.
YAHAGI.	Sasebo Navy yd.	11-11-41.	25-10-42.	29-12-43.

Fate: Sunk. 07-04-45. After seriously damaged by bombs. By US Navy A/c.

Name.	Builder.	Laid dwn.	Launched.	Completed.
SAKAWA.	As above.	21-11-42.	09-04-44.	30-11-44.

Fate: Sunk. 02-07-46. In A-Tests at Bikini Attoll.

LIGHT CRUISERS.
(Ex Chinese).

Displacement: 2,500 Tonnes.　　　　Complement: 340.

Dimensions:　360'0" x 29'0" x 13'0".

Machinery:　4 Boilers, 2 Shaft geared turbines. 9,500Shp = 22Kts.

Fuel Cap:　(Oil) Unknown.

Armour:　Deck. 1.0", Turrets. 1.0".

Armament:　6 x 5.5", 6 x 3.0" AA, 4 x 21"TT, A/c Never fitted.

Name.	Builder.	Laid dwn.	Launched.	Completed.
IOSHIMA.	Harima Co, Harima.	1930.	10-10-31.	1932.

Ex NING HAI.

Fate: Sunk. 19-04-44. Torpedoed by US.S/m SHAD. off Honshu.

Name.	Builder.	Laid dwn.	Launched.	Completed.
YASOSHIMA.	Kiangnan Shanghai.	09-07-31.	29-09-35.	18-06-36.

Ex PING HAI.

Fate: Sunk.25-11-44. Bombed by US Navy A/c at Luzon.

OYODO (Class).

Displacement: 11,433 Tonnes.　　　　Complement: Unknown.

Dimensions:　630'3" x 54'6" x 19'6".

Machinery:　6 Boilers, 4 Shaft geared turbines. 110,000Shp = 35Kts.

Fuel Cap:　(Oil) Unknown.

Armour:　Belt. 2.0", Deck. 1.4", Turrets. 1.0".

Armament:　6 x 1.0", 8 x 3.9" AA, 12 x 25mm AA, TT None fitted.

Name.	Builder.	Laid dwn.	Launched.	Completed.
OYODO.	Kure Navy yd.	14-02-41.	02-04-42.	28-02-43.

Fate: Sunk. 28-07-45. Bombed by US Navy A/c in shallow water at Kure. BU 1948.

DESTROYERS.

MUTSUKI (Class).

Displacment: 14,045 Tonnes. **Complement:** 150.
Dimensions: 328'9" x 20'0" x 9'9".
Machinery: 4 Boilers, 2 Shaft geared turbines. 38,000Shp = 37.2Kts.
Fuel Cap: (Oil) Unknown.
Armour: None.
Armament: 4 x 4.7", 2 x 7.7mm MG AA, 6 x 24"TT, 18 DC.

Name.	Builder.	Laid dwn.	Launched.	Completed.
MITSUKI.	Sasebo Navy yd.	1924.	23-07-25.	Unknown.

Fate: Sunk. 25-08-42. Battle for the Solomans.

Name.	Builder.	Laid dwn.	Launched.	Completed.
KISAGARI.	Maizuru Navy yd.	1924.	05-06-25.	Unknown.

Fate: Sunk. 11-12-41. Cause unknown.

Name.	Builder.	Laid dwn.	Launched.	Completed.
YAYOI.	Urago Tokyo.	1924.	11-07-25.	Unknown.

Fate: Sunk. 11-09-42. Battle for the Solomans.

Name.	Builder.	Laid dwn.	Launched.	Completed.
UDZUKI.	Ishikawajima Tokyo.	1924.	15-10-25.	Unknown.

Fate: Sunk. 12-02-44. Torpedoed by US. PT Boats.

Name.	Builder.	Laid dwn.	Launched.	Completed.
SATSUKI.	Fujinagata Osaka.	1924.	25-03-25.	Unknown.

Fate: Sunk. 21-09-44. Cause unknown.

Name.	Builder.	Laid dwn.	Launched.	Completed.
MINADSUKI.	Uraga Tokyo.	1924.	25-05--25.	Unknown.

Fate: Sunk. 06-06-44. Torpedoed by US. S/m. Name Unknown.

Name.	Builder.	Laid dwn.	Launched.	Completed.
FUMINDSUKI.	Fujinagata Osaka.	1924.	16-02-26.	Unknown.

Fate: Sunk. 18-02-44. Cause unknown.

Name.	Builder.	Laid dwn.	Launched.	Completed.
NAGATSUKI.	Ishikainajima Tokyo.	1924.	06-10-26.	Unknown.

Fate: Sunk. 06-07-44. Cause Unknown.

Name.	Builder.	Laid dwn.	Launched.	Completed.
KIKUDSUKI.	Maizuru Navy yd.	1924.	15-05-26.	Unknown.

Fate: Sunk. 04-05-42. Battle for the Solomans.

Name.	Builder.	Laid dwn.	Launched.	Completed.
MIKADSUKI.	Sasebo Navy yd.	1924.	12-07-26.	Unknown.

Fate: Sunk. 28-07-43. Battle for the Solomans.

Name.	Builder.	Laid dwn.	Launched.	Completed.
MOCHIDSUKI.	Urago Tokyo.	1924.	12-07-26.	Unknown.

Fate: Sunk. 12-12-44. Cause unknown

DESTROYERS. (Continued).

MUTSUKI. Class. (Continued).

Name.	Builder.	Laid dwn.	Launched.	Completed.
YUDSUKI.	Fujinagata Osaka.	1924.	04-03-27.	Unknown.

Fate: Sunk.12-12-44. Cause unknown.

FUBUKI (Class).

Displacement: 2,057 Tonnes.   Complement: 197.
Dimensions: 388'6" x 34'0" x 10'6".
Machinery: 4 Boilers. 2 Shaft geared turbines. 50,000Shp = 38Kts.
Fuel Cap: Oil. 500 Tons.
Armour: None.
Armament: 6 x 5.0", 2 x 13mm, 9 x 24"TT, 18 DC.

Name.	Builder.	Laid dwn.	Launched.	Completed.
FUBUKI.	Maizuru Navy yd.	Unknown.	15-11-27.	Unknown.

Fate: Sunk. 11-10-42. By US Naval gunfire.

Name.	Builder.	Laid dwn.	Launched.	Completed.
AYANAMI.	Fujinagata Osaka.	Unknown.	05-10-29.	Unknown.

Fate: Sunk. 15-11-42. By US Naval gunfire.

Name.	Builder.	Laid dwn.	Launched.	Completed.
YUGIRI..	Maizuru Navy yd.	Unknown.	12-05-30.	Unknown.

Fate: Sunk. 25-11-42. By US Naval gunfire.

Name.	Builder.	Laid dwn.	Launched.	Completed.
MIYUKI.	Uraga Tokyo.	Unknown.	26-06-28.	Unknown.

Fate: Sunk,29-06-34. with destroyer INAUMA.

Name.	Builder.	Laid dwn.	Launched.	Completed.
SHINONOME.	Sasebo Navy yd.	Unknown.	26-11-27.	Unknown.

Fate: Sunk 18-12-41. Mined.

Name.	Builder.	Laid dwn.	Launched.	Completed.
AMAGIRI.	Isikawajima Tokyo.	Unknown.	27-02-30.	Unknown.

Fate: Sunk. 23-04-44. Mined.

Name.	Builder.	Laid dwn.	Launched.	Completed.
SAGIRI.	Uraga Tokyo.	Unknown.	23-12-39.	Unknown.

Fate: Sunk.24-12-41. Torpedoed by Dutch S/M.

Name.	Builder.	Laid dwn.	Launched.	Completed.
USUGUMO.	Ishikawajima Tokyo.	Unknown.	26-12-27.	Unknown.

Fate: Sunk. 07-07-44. Torpedoed by US S/m..

Name.	Builder.	Laid dwn.	Launched.	Completed.
SHIRAKUMO.	Fujinagata Osaka.	Unknown.	27-12-27.	Unknown.

Fate: Sunk. 16-03-44. Torpedoed by US S/m.

DESTROYERS. (Continued).

FUBUKI Class, (Continued).

Name.	Builder.	Laid dwn.	Launched.	Completed.
ISONAMI.	Uraga Tokyo.	Unknown,	24-11-27.	Unknown.

Fate: Sunk. 09-04-44. Torpedoed by US S/m.

Name.	Builder.	Laid dwn.	Launched.	Completed.
SHIKINAMI.	Maizuru Navy yd.	Unknown.	22-06-29.	Unknown.

Fate: Sunk. 12-09-44. Torpedoed by US S/m.

Name.	Builder.	Laid dwn.	Launched.	Completed.
SASANAMI.	Maizuru Navy yd.	Unknown.	06-06-31.	Unknown.

Fate: Sunk. 14-01-44. Torpedoed by US S/m.

Name.	Builder.	Laid dwn.	Launched.	Completed.
SHIRAYUKI.	Yokohama Co.	Unknown.	20-03-28.	Unknown.

Fate: Sunk. 03-03-43. By US A/c.

Name.	Builder.	Laid dwn.	Launched.	Completed.
HATSUYUKI.	Maizuru Navy yd.	Unknown.	29-09-27.	Unknown.

Fate: Sunk. 17-07-43. By US A/c.

Name.	Builder.	Laid dwn.	Launched.	Completed.
MURAKUMO.	Fujinagata Osaka.	Unknown.	27-09-27.	Unknown.

Fate: Sunk. 12-10-42. By US A/c.

Name.	Builder.	Laid dwn.	Launched.	Completed.
URINAMI.	Sasebo Navy yd.	Unknown.	29-11-28.	Unknown.

Fate: Sunk. 26-10-44. By US A/c..

Name.	Builder.	Laid dwn.	Launched.	Completed.
ASAGIRI.	Sasebo Navy yd.	Unknown.	18-11-29.	Unknown.

Fate: Sunk. 28-08-42. By US A/c.

Name.	Builder.	Laid dwn.	Launched.	Completed.
OBORO.	Sasebo Navy yd.	Unknown.	09-11-30.	Unknown.

Fate: Sunk. 16-10-42. By US A/c.

Name.	Builder.	Laid dwn.	Launched.	Completed.
AKEBONO.	Fujinagata Osaka.	Unknown.	07-11-30.	Unknown.

Fate: Sunk. 13-11-44. By US A/c.

Name.	Builder.	Laid dwn.	Launched.	Completed.
USHIO.	Uraga Tokyo.	Unknown.	17-11-30.	Unknown.

Fate: Sunk. By US A/c. Date unknown.

DESTROYERS. (Continued).

AKATSUKI (Class).

Displacement: 1,950 Tonnes.   Compliment: 197.
Dimensions: 371'9" x 34'0" x 10'9"
Machinery: 3 Boilers. 2 Shaft geared turbines. 50,000Shp = 38Kts.
Fuel Cap: Oil. 475 Tons.
Armour: None.
Armament: 6 x 5.0", 2 x 13mmAA, 9 x 24"TT, 14 DC.

Name.	Builder.	Laid dwn.	Launched.	Completed.
AKATSUKI.	Sasebo Navy yd.	Unknown.	07-05-32.	Unknown.

Fate: Sunk. 13-11-42. By gunfire at Guadalcanal.

Name.	Builder.	Laid dwn.	Launched.	Completed.
HIBIKI.	Maizuru Navy yd.	Unknown.	16-06-32.	Unknown.

Fate: To USSR 1947, renamed PRITKY. BU 1963.

Name.	Builder.	Laid dwn.	Launched.	Completed.
INAZUCHI.	Uraga Tokyo.	Unknown.	22-10-31.	Unknown.

Fate: Sunk. 14-04-44. Torpedoed by US S/m.

Name.	Builder.	Laid dwn.	Launched.	Completed.
INAZUMA.	Fujinagata Osaka.	Unknown.	25-02-32.	

Fate: Sunk. 14-05-44. Torpedoed by US S/m.

HATSUHARU (Class).

Displacement: 1,802 Tonnes.   Compliment: 200.
Dimensions: 359'3" x 32'10" x 9'11".
Machinery: 3 Boilers. 2 Shaft geared turbines. 42,000Shp = 36.5Kts.
Fuel Cap: Oil. 500 Tons.
Armour: None.
Armament: 5 x 5.0", 2 x 13mmAA, 9 x 24"TT, 14 DC.

Name.	Builder.	Laid dwn.	Launched.	Completed.
HATSUHARU.	Sasebo Navy yd.	Unknown.	27-02-33.	Unknown.

Fate: Sunk. 12-11-44. Torpedoed by US S/m.

Name.	Builder.	Laid dwn.	Launched.	Completed.
NENOHI.	Uraga Tokyo.	Unknown.	04-11-33.	Unknown.

Fate: Sunk. 04-07-42. By US A/c.

Name.	Builder.	Laid dwn.	Launched.	Completed.
HATSUSHIMO.	Uraga Tokyo.	Unknown.	04-11-33.	Unknown.

Fate: Sunk. 30-07-45. Mined.

Name.	Builder.	Laid dwn.	Launched.	Completed.
WAKABA.	Sasebo Navy yd.	Unknown.	18-03-34.	Unknown.

Fate: Sunk. 24-10-44. By US A/c.

DESTROYERS. (Continued).

HATSUHARU (Class). (Continued).

Name.	Builder.	Laid dwn.	Launched.	Completed.
YUGURE.	Maizuru Navy yd.	Unknown.	06-05-34.	Unknown

Fate: Sunk. 20-07-43. By US A/c.

Name.	Builder.	Laid dwn.	Launched.	Completed.
ARIAKE.	Kawasaki Kobe.	Unknown.	23-09-34.	Unknown.

Fate: Sunk. 28-07-43.

SHIRATSUYU (Class).

Displacement: 1,950 Tonnes.   Compliment: 180.
Dimensions: 352'8" x 32'6" x 11'6".
Machinery: 3 Boilers. 2 Shaft geared turbines. 42,000Shp = 34.0Kts.
Fuel Cap: Oil. 500 Tons.
Armour: None.
Armament: 5 x 5.0", 2 x 13mmAA, 8 x 24"TT, 16 DC.

Name.	Builder.	Laid dwn.	Launched.	Completed.
SHIRATSUYU.	Sasebo Navy yd.	Unknown.	05-04-35.	Unknown.

Fate: Sunk. 05-06-44. After collision with a tanker.

Name.	Builder.	Laid dwn.	Launched.	Completed.
SHIGURE.	Uraga Tokyo.	Unknown.	18-05-35.	Unknown.

Fate: Sunk. 24-01-45. Torpedoed by US S/m.

Name.	Builder.	Laid dwn.	Launched.	Completed.
MURASAME.	Fujinagata Osaka.	Unknown.	20-06-35.	Unknown.

Fate: Sunk. 06-03-43. After action with US surface ships.

Name.	Builder.	Laid dwn.	Launched.	Completed.
YUDACHI.	Sasebo Navy yd.	Unknown.	21-06-36.	Unknown.

Fate: Sunk. 13-11-42. After action with US surface ships.

Name.	Builder.	Laid dwn.	Launched.	Completed.
KAWAKAZE.	Fujinagata Osaka.	Unknown.	01-11-36.	Unknown.

Fate: Sunk. 06-08-43. After action with US surface ships.

Name.	Builder.	Laid dwn.	Launched.	Completed.
HARUSAME.	Uraga Tokyo.	Unknown.	21-09-35.	Unknown.

Fate: Sunk. 08-06-44. By US A/c.

Name.	Builder.	Laid dwn.	Launched.	Completed.
SUZAKAZE.	Uraga Tokyo.	Unknown.	11-03-37.	Unknown.

Fate: Sunk. 26-01-44. Torpedoed by US S/m.

Name.	Builder.	Laid dwn.	Launched.	Completed.
UMIKAZE.	Maizuru Navy yd.	Unknown.	27-11-36.	Unknown.

Fate: Sunk. 01-02-44. Torpedoed by US S/m.

DESTROYERS. (Continued).

SHIRATSUYU (Class). (Continued).

Name.	Builder.	Laid dwn.	Launched.	Completed.
YAMAKAZE.	Uraga Tokyo.	Unknown.	21-02-36.	Unknown.

Fate: Sunk. 25-06-36. Torpedoed by US S/m.

Name.	Builder.	Laid dwn.	Launched.	Completed.
SAMIDARE.	Uraga Tokyo.	Unknown.	06-07-35.	Unknown.

Fate: Sunk. Torpedoed by US S/m.

ASASHIO (Class).

Displacement: 2,330 Tonnes.   Compliment: 200.
Dimensions: 388'0" x 33'11" x 12'1".
Machinery: 3 Boilers, 2 Shaft geared turbines. 50,000Shp = 35.0Kts.
Fuel Cap: Oil. 500 Tons.
Armour: None.
Armament: 6 x 5.0", 4 x 5mmAA, 8 x 24"TT, 16 DC.

Name.	Builder.	Laid dwn.	Launched.	Completed.
OSHIO.	Maizuru Navy yd.	Unknown.	19-04-37.	Unknown.

Fate: Sunk. 20-02-43. Torpedoed by US S/m.

Name.	Builder.	Laid dwn.	Launched.	Completed.
ARARE.	Maizuru Navy yd.	Unknown.	19-04-37.	Unknown.

Fate: Sunk. 05-07-42. Torpedoed by US S/m.

Name.	Builder.	Laid dwn.	Launched.	Completed.
MICHISHIO.	Fujinagata Osaka.	Unknown.	15-03-37.	Unknown.

Fate: Sunk. 25-10-44. By US ships during the Battle of Surigao Straits.

Name.	Builder.	Laid dwn.	Launched.	Completed.
YAMAGUMO.	Fujinagata Osaka.	Unknown.	24-07-37.	Unknown.

Fate: Sunk. 25-10-44. By US ships during the Battle of Surigao Straits.

Name.	Builder.	Laid dwn.	Launched.	Completed.
ASAGUMO.	Kawasaki Kobe.	Unknown.	05-11-37.	Unknown.

Fate: Sunk. 25-10-44. By US ships during the battle of Surigao Straits.

Name.	Builder.	Laid dwn.	Launched.	Completed.
MINEGUMO.	Fujinagata Osaka.	Unknown.	04-11-37.	Unknown.

Fate: Sunk. 25-05-43. By US ships.

Name.	Builder.	Laid dwn.	Launched.	Completed.
ASASHIO.	Sasebo Navy yd.	Unknown.	16-12-36.	Unknown.

Fate: Sunk. 04-03-43. By US Navy & Land basedA/c.

Name.	Builder.	Laid dwn.	Launched.	Completed.
ARASHIO.	Kawasaki Kobe.	Unknown.	26-05-37.	Unknown.

Fate: Sunk. 04-03-43. By US Navy & Land based A/c.

DESTROYERS. (Continued).

ASASHIO. (Class). (Continued).

Name.	Builder.	Laid dwn.	Launched.	Completed.
NATSUGUMO.	Sasebo Navy yd.	Unknown.	26-05-37	Unknown.

Fate. Sunk. 12-10-42. By US Navy & Land based A/c.

Name.	Builder.	Laid dwn.	Launched.	Completed.
KISUMI.	Uraga Tokyo.	Unknown.	18-11-37.	Unknown.

Fate: Sunk. 07-04-45. By US Navy & Land based A/c.

KAGERO (Class).

Displacement: 2,450 Tonnes.   Compliment: 240.
Dimensions: 388'9" x 35'5" x 12'4"
Machinery: 3 Boilers, 2 Shaft geared turbines. 52,000Shp = 35Kts.
Fuel Cap: Oil. Unknown.
Armour: None.
Armament: 6 x 5.0", 4 x 25mmAA, 8 x 24"TT, 16 DC.

Name.	Builder.	Laid dwn.	Launched.	Completed.
KAGERO.	Maizuru Navy yd.	Unknown.	27-09-38.	Unknown.

Fate: Sunk. 08-05-43. By US Navy & Land based A/c.

Name.	Builder.	Laid dwn.	Launched.	Completed.
OYAHIO.	Maizuru Navy yd.	Unknown.	29-11-38.	Unknown.

Fate: Sunk. 08-05-43. By US Navy & Land based A/c.

Name.	Builder.	Laid dwn.	Launched.	Completed.
YUKIZAZE.	Sasebo Navy yd.	Unknown.	24-03-39.	Unknown.

Fate: To China 1947. Renamed TAN YANG.

Name.	Builder.	Laid dwn.	Launched.	Completed.
HAYASHIO.	Uraga Tokyo.	Unknown.	19-04-39.	Unknown.

Fate: Sunk. 24-11-42. By US Navy & Land based A/c.

Name.	Builder.	Laid dwn.	Launched.	Completed.
ISOKAZE.	Sasebo Navy yd.	Unknown.	19-06-39.	Unknown.

Fate: Sunk. 07-04-45. by US Navy & Land based A/c.

Name.	Builder.	Laid dwn.	Launched.	Completed.
SHIRANUI.	Uraga Tokyo.	Unknown.	28-06-38.	Unknown.

Fate: Sunk. 27-10-44. By US Navy & Land based A/c.

Name.	Builder.	Laid dwn.	Launched.	Completed.
AMATSUKAZE.	Maizuru Navy yd.	Unknown.	19-10-39.	Unknown.

Fate: Sunk. 06-04-45. By US Navy & Land based A/c.

Name.	Builder.	Laid dwn.	Launched.	Completed.
TOKITSUKAZE.	Uraga Tokyo.	Unknown.	10-11-39.	Unknown.

Fate: Sunk. 03-03-43. By US Navy & Land based A/c.

DESTROYERS. (Continued).

KAGERO (Class). (Continued).

Name.	Builder.	Laid dwn.	Launched.	Completed.
HAMAKAZE.	Uraga Tokyo.	Unknown.	25-11-40.	Unknown.

Fate: Sunk. 07-04-45. By US Navy & Land based A/c.

Name.	Builder.	Laid dwn.	Launched.	Completed.
KUROSHIO.	Fujinagata Osaka.	Unknown.	25-10-38.	Unknown.

Fate: Sunk. 07-05-43. Mined.

Name.	Builder.	Laid dwn.	Launched.	Completed.
NATSUSHIO.	Fujinagata Osaka.	Unknown.	23-02-39.	Unknown.

Fate: Sunk. 08-02-42. Torpedoed by US S/m.

Name.	Builder.	Laid dwn.	Launched.	Completed.
URAKAZE.	Fujinagata Osaka.	Unknown.	19-04-40.	Unknown.

Fate: Sunk. 21-11-44. Torpedoed by US S/m.

Name.	Builder.	Laid dwn.	Launched.	Completed.
TANIKAZE.	Fujinagata Osaka.	Unknown.	01-11-40.	Unknown.

Fate: Sunk. 09-06-44. Torpedoed by US S/m.

Name.	Builder.	Laid dwn.	Launched.	Completed.
HATSUKAZE.	Kawasaki Kobe.	Unknown.	24-01-39.	Unknown.

Fate: Sunk. 02-11-43. By US Navy ships.

Name.	Builder.	Laid dwn.	Launched.	Completed.
MAIKAZE.	Fujinagata Osaka.	Unknown.	15-03-41.	Unknown.

Fate: Sunk. 17-02-44. By US Navy ships.

Name.	Builder.	Laid dwn.	Launched.	Completed.
NOWAKI.	Maizuru Navy yd.	Unknown.	17-09-40.	Unknown.

Fate: Sunk. 26-11-44. By US Navy ships.

Name.	Builder.	Laid dwn.	Launched.	Completed.
ARASHI.	Maizuru Navy yd.	Unknown.	22-04-40.	Unknown.

Fate: Sunk. 07-08-43. By US Navy ships.

Name.	Builder.	Laid dwn.	Launched.	Completed.
HAGAKAZE.	Uraga Tokyo.	Unknown.	18-06-40.	Unknown.

Fate: Sunk. 07-08-43. By US Navy ships.

DESTROYERS. (Continued).

YUGUMO (Class).

Displacement:	2,480 Tonnes.	Compliment: 228.
Dimensions:	391'0" x 35'5" x 12'4".	
Machinery:	3 Boilers, 2 Shaft geared turbines. 52,000Shp = 35.0Kts.	
Fuel Cap:	Unknown.	
Armour:	None.	
Armament:	6 x 5.0", 4 x 25mmAA, 8 x 24"TT, 36 DC.	

Name.	Builder.	Laid dwn.	Launched.	Completed.
YUGUMO.	Maizuru Navy yd.	Unknown.	16-03-41.	Unknown.

Fate: Sunk. 06-11-43. By US Navy ships.

Name.	Builder.	Laid dwn.	Launched.	Completed.
MAKINAMI.	Maizuru Navy yd.	Unknown.	27-12-41.	Unknown.

Fate: Sunk. 25-11-43. By US Navy ships.

Name.	Builder.	Laid dwn.	Launched.	Completed.
TAKINAMI.	Uraga Tokyo.	Unknown.	16-03-42.	Unknown.

Fate: Sunk. 01-12-42. By US Navy ships.

Name.	Builder.	Laid dwn.	Launched.	Completed.
ONAMI.	Fujinagata Osaka.	Unknown.	31-08-42.	Unknown.

Fate: Sunk. 25-11-43. By US Navy ships.

Name.	Builder.	Laid dwn.	Launched.	Completed.
MAKINUMO.	Fujinagata Osaka.	Unknown.	05-11-41.	Unknown.

Fate: Sunk. 01-02-43. Mined.

Name.	Builder.	Laid dwn.	Launched.	Completed.
AKIGUMO.	Urago Tokyo.	Unknown.	11-04-41.	Unknown.

Fate: Sunk. 11-04-44. Torpedoed by US S/m.

Name.	Builder.	Laid dwn.	Launched.	Completed.
KAZEKUMO.	Urago Tokyo.	Unknown.	26-09-41.	Unknown.

Fate: Sunk. 08-06-44. Torpedoed by US S/m.

Name.	Builder.	Laid dwn.	Launched.	Completed.
TAMANAMI.	Fujinagata Osaka.	Unknown.	20-12-42.	Unknown.

Fate: Sunk. 20-12-44. Torpedoed by US S/m.

Name.	Builder.	Laid dwn.	Launched.	Completed.
KISHINAMI.	Uraga Tokyo.	Unknown.	19-08-43.	Unknown.

Fate: Sunk. 04-12-44. Torpedoed by US S/m.

Name.	Builder.	Laid dwn.	Launched.	Completed.
HAYANAMI.	Maizuru Navy yd.	Unknown.	19-12-42.	Unknown.

Fate: Sunk. 07-06-44. Torpedoed by US S/m.

DESTROYERS. (Continued).

YUGUMO (Class). (Continued).

Name.	Builder.	Laid dwn.	Launched.	Completed.
KIOSHIMO.	Uraga Tokyo.	Unknown.	29-02-44.	Unknown.

Fate: Sunk. 26-12-44. Torpedoed by US PT Boat.

Name.	Builder.	Laid dwn.	Launched.	Completed.
AKISHIMO.	Fujinagata Osaka.	Unknown.	05-12-43.	Unknown.

Fate: Sunk. 13-11-44.

Name.	Builder.	Laid dwn.	Launched.	Completed.
NAGANAMI.	Fujinagata Osaka.	Unknown.	05-03-42.	Unknown.

Fate: Sunk. 11-11-44.

Name.	Builder.	Laid dwn.	Launched.	Completed.
SUZANAMI.	Uraga Tokyo.	Unknown.	12-03-43.	Unknown.

Fate: Sunk. 11-11-43.

Name.	Builder.	Laid dwn.	Launched.	Completed.
FUJINAMI.	Fujinagata Osaka.	Unknown.	20-11-43.	Unknown.

Fate: Sunk. 27-10-44.

Name.	Builder.	Laid dwn.	Launched.	Completed.
KIYONAMI.	Uraga Tokyo.	Unknown.	17-08-42.	Unknown.

Fate: Sunk. 20-07-43.

Name.	Builder.	Laid dwn.	Launched.	Completed.
OKINAMI.	Maizuru Navy yd.	Unknown.	18-07-43.	Unknown.

Fate: Sunk. 13-11-44.

Name.	Builder.	Laid dwn.	Launched.	Completed.
HAMANAMI.	Maizuru Navy yd.	Unknown.	18-04-43.	Unknown.

Fate: Sunk. 11-11-44.

Name.	Builder.	Laid dwn.	Launched.	Completed.
ASAHIMO.	Fujinagata Osaka.	Unknown.	18-07-43.	Unknown.

Fate: Sunk. 07-04-45.

Name.	Builder.	Laid dwn.	Launched.	Completed.
HAYASHIMO.	Maizuru Navy yd.	Unknown.	xx-11-43.	Unknown.

Fate: Sunk. 26-10-44.

DESTROYERS. (Continued).

SHIMAKAZE. (Class).

Displacement: 1,300 Tonnes.   Compliment: Unknown..

Dimensions: 413'5" x 36'9" x 13'7"

Machinery. 3 Boilers, 2 Shaft geared turbines. 75,000Shp = 39Kts.

Fuel Cap: Oil. Unknown.

Armour: None.

Armament: 6 x 5.0", 4 x 13.2mmAA, 26 x 25mmAA, 15 x 24"TT, 18 DC.

Name.	Builder.	Laid dwn.	Launched.	Completed.
SHIMAKAZE.	Maizuru Navy yd.	Unknown.	18-07-42.	Unknown.

Fate: Sunk. 11-11-42. By US Navy A/c, off Cebu, Phillipines.

AKITSUKI. (Class).

Displacement: Unknown Tonnes.   Compliment: 300.

Dimensions: 440'3" x 38'91 x 13'7"

Machinery: 3 Boilers, 2 Shaft geared turbines. 52,000Shp = 33Kts.

Fuel Cap: Oil. 1,097 Tons.

Armour: None.

Armament: 8 x 3.9", 40 x 25mmAA, 4 x 24"TT, 72 DC.

Name.	Builder.	Laid dwn.	Launched.	Completed.
AKITSUKI.	Maizuru Navy yd.	Unknown.	02-07-41.	Unknown.

Fate: Sunk. 25-10-44. By US Navy A/c.

Name.	Builder.	Laid dwn.	Launched.	Completed.
WAKATSUKI.	Mitsubishi Nagasaki.	Unknown.	24-11-42.	Unknown.

Fate: Sunk. 11-11-44. By US Navy A/c.

Name.	Builder.	Laid dwn.	Launched.	Completed.
SIMOTSUKI.	Unknown.	Unknown.	Unknown.	Unknown.

Fate: Sunk. Date Unknown. Torpedoed by US S/m.

Name.	Builder.	Laid dwn.	Launched.	Completed.
TERUTSUKI.	Mitsubishi Nagasaki.	Unknown.	21-11-41.	Unknown.

Fate: Sunk. 12-12-42. Torpedoed by US PT Boats.

Name.	Builder.	Laid dwn.	Launched.	Completed.
HATSUSUKI.	Maizuru Navy yd.	Unknown.	03-04-42.	Unknown.

Fate: Sunk. 25-10-44. BY US Navy ships.

Name.	Builder.	Laid dwn.	Launched.	Completed.
MITSUKI.	Mitsubishi Nagasaki.	Unknown.	29-06-42.	Unknown.

Fate: Sunk. 06-07-43. By US Navy ships.

Name.	Builder.	Laid dwn.	Launched.	Completed.
SHIMOTSUKI.	Mitsubishi Nagasaki.	Unknown.	07-04-43.	Unknown.

Fate: Sunk. 25-11-44. By US Navy ships.

DESTROYERS. (Continued).

AKITSUKI. (Class). (Continued).

Name.	Builder.	Laid dwn.	Launched.	Completed.
YOITSUKI.	Uraga Tokyo.	Unknown.	25-09-44.	Unknown.

Fate: To China 1947. Renamed FEN YANG. BU 1963.

Name.	Builder.	Laid dwn.	Launched.	Completed.
HARATSUKI.	Sasebo Navy yd.	Unknown.	03-08-44.	Unknown.

Fate: To USSR 1947.

MATSU (Class. Escort Type).

Displacement: 1,506 Tonnes.	Compliment: Unknown.

Dimensions: 328'1" x 30'8" x 10'10".
Machinery: 2 Boilers, 2 Shaft geared turbines. 19,000Shp = 27.0Kts.
Fuel Cap: Unknown.
Armour: None.
Armament: 3 x 5.0", 28 x25mmAA, 4 x 24"TT, 36 DC.

Name.	Builder.	Laid dwn.	Launched.	Completed.
MATSU.	Maizuru Navy yd.	Unknown.	03-02-44.	Unknown.

Fate: Sunk. 04-08-44. Cause unknown.

Name.	Builder.	Laid dwn.	Launched.	Completed.
UME.	Fujinagata Osaka.	Unknown.	24-04-44.	Unknown.

Fate: Sunk. 31-01-45. Cause unknown.

Name.	Builder.	Laid dwn.	Launched.	Completed.
KUWA.	Fujinagata Osaka.	Unknown.	25-05-44.	Unknown.

Fate: Sunk. 03-12-44. Cause unknown.

Name.	Builder.	Laid dwn.	Launched.	Completed.
MOMI.	Yokosuka Navy yd.	Unknown.	16-06-44.	Unknown.

Fate: Sunk. Cause unknown.

Name.	Builder.	Laid dwn.	Launched.	Completed.
HINOKI.	Yokosuka Navy yd.	Unknown.	04-07-44.	Unknown.

Fate: Sunk. 07-01-45. Cause unknown.

Name.	Builder.	Laid dwn.	Launched.	Completed.
MOMO.	Maizuru Navy yd.	Unknown.	23-03-44.	Unknown.

Fate: Sunk. 15-12-44. Torpedoed by US S/m.

Name.	Builder.	Laid dwn.	Launched.	Completed.
SAKURA.	Yokosuka Navy yd.	Unknown.	06-09-44.	Unknown.

Fate: Sunk. Mined.

Name.	Builder.	Laid dwn.	Launched.	Completed.
TAKE.	Yokosuka Navy yd.	Unknown.	28-03-44.	Unknown.

Fate: To UK. BU 1947.

DESTROYERS. (Continued).

MATSU (Class. Escort Type). (Continued).

Name.	Builder.	Laid dwn.	Launched.	Completed.
MAKI.	Maizuru Navy yd.	Unknown.	10-06-44.	Unknown

Fate: To UK. BU 1947.

Name.	Builder.	Laid dwn.	Launched.	Completed.
KIRI.	Yokosuka Navy yd.	Unknown.	27-05-44.	Unknown.

Fate: To USSR 1947.

Name.	Builder.	Laid dwn.	Launched.	Completed.
KAYA.	Maizuru Navy yd.	Unknown.	30-07-44.	Unknown.

Fate: To USSR 1947.

Name.	Builder.	Laid dwn.	Launched.	Completed.
KAEDE.	Yokosuka Navy yd.	Unknown.	25-07-44.	Unknown.

Fate: To China 1947. Renamed HEN YANG.

Name.	Builder.	Laid dwn.	Launched.	Completed.
KEYAKI.	Yokosuka Navy yd.	Unknown.	30-09-44.	Unknown.

Fate: To USA 1947. Expended as target.

Name.	Builder.	Laid dwn.	Launched.	Completed.
NARA.	Fujinagata Osaka.	Unknown.	12-10-44.	Unknown.

Fate: BU 1948.

Name.	Builder.	Laid dwn.	Launched.	Completed.
TSUBAKI.	Maizuru Navy yd.	Unknown.	30-09-44.	Unknown.

Fate: BU 1948.

Name.	Builder.	Laid dwn.	Launched.	Completed.
YUNAGI.	Fujinagata Osaka.	Unknown.	25-11-44.	Unknown.

Fate: BU 1947.

TACHIBANA (Class. Escort Type).

Displacement: 1,555 Tonnes.	Compliment: Unknown.

Dimensions: 328'1" x 30'8" x 11'1".
Machinery: 2 Boilers, 2 Shaft geared turbines. 19,000Shp = 27.8Kts.
Fuel Cap: Unknown.
Armour: None.
Armament: 3 x 5.0", 24 x 25mmAA, 4 x 24"TT, 60 DC.

Name.	Builder.	Laid dwn.	Launched.	Completed.
TACHIBANA.	Yokosuka Navy yd.	Unknown.	14-10-44.	Unknown.

Fate: Sunk. 14-07-45. By US Navy A/c.

Name.	Builder.	Laid dwn.	Launched.	Completed.
NASHI.	Kawasaki Kobe.	Unknown.	17-01-45.	Unknown.

Fate: Sunk. 28-07-45. By US Navy A/c.

DESTROYERS. (Continued).

TACHIBANA (Class). (Continued).

Name.	Builder.	Laid dwn.	Launched.	Completed.
ENOKI.	Maizuru Navy yd.	Unknown.	27-01-45.	Unknown.

Fate: Sunk. 26-06-45. Mined in shallow water. Salvaged and scrapped after the war.

Name.	Builder.	Laid dwn.	Launched.	Completed.
TSUTA.	Yokosuka Navy yd.	Unknown.	02-11-44.	Unknown.

Fate: To CHINA. 1947. Renamed HUA YANG.

Name.	Builder.	Laid dwn.	Launched.	Completed.
HATSUYUME.	Maizuru Navy yd.	Unknown.	25-05-45.	Unknown.

Fate: To CHINA. 1947. Renamed HSIN YANG.

Name.	Builder.	Laid dwn.	Launched.	Completed.
HAGI.	Yokosuka Navy yd.	Unknown.	27-11-45.	Unknown.

Fate: To UK. 1947. BU.

Name.	Builder.	Laid dwn.	Launched.	Completed.
SUMIRE.	Yokosuka Navy yd.	Unknown.	27-12-44.	Unknown.

Fate: To UK. 1947. Expended as target.

Name.	Builder.	Laid dwn.	Launched.	Completed.
KUSONOKI.	Yokosuka Navy yd.	Unknown.	18-01-45.	Unknown.

Fate: To UK. 1947. BU.

Name.	Builder.	Laid dwn.	Launched.	Completed.
KAKI.	Yokosuka Navy yd.	Unknown.	11-12-44.	Unknown.

Fate: To USA. 1947. BU.

Name.	Builder.	Laid dwn.	Launched.	Completed.
ODAKI.	Maizuru Navy yd.	Unknown.	10-03-45.	Unknown.

Fate: To USA. 1947. BU.

Name.	Builder.	Laid dwn.	Launched.	Completed.
KABA.	Fujinagata Osaka.	Unknown.	27-02-45.	Unknown.

Fate: To USA. 1947. BU.

Name.	Builder.	Laid dwn.	Launched.	Completed.
SHII.	Maizuru Navy yd.	Unknown.	13-01-45.	Unknown.

Fate: To USSR. 1947.

Name.	Builder.	Laid dwn.	Launched.	Completed.
HATSUZAKURA.	Yokosuka Navy yd.	Unknown.	20-02-45.	Unknown.

Fate: To USSR. 1947.

Name.	Builder.	Laid dwn.	Launched.	Completed.
NIRE.	Yokosuka Navy yd.	Unknown.	25-11-44.	Unknown.

Fate: BU. 1948.

DESTROYERS. (Continued).

TACHIBANA (Class). (Continued).

Name.	Builder.	Laid dwn.	Launched.	Completed.
WAKARAKURA.	Fujinagata Osaka.	Unknown.	Unknown	Unknown.

Fate. BU. 1945.

Name.	Builder.	Laid dwn.	Launched.	Completed.
AZUSA.	Yokosuka Navy yd.	Unknown.	Unknown.	Unknown.

Fate: BU. 1945.

Name.	Builder.	Laid dwn.	Launched.	Completed.
SAKAKI.	Yokosuka Navy yd.	Unknown.	Unknown.	Unknown.

Fate: BU. 1945.

Name.	Builder.	Laid dwn.	Launched.	Completed.
KUZU.	Yokosuka Navy yd.	Unknown.	Unknown.	Unknown

Fate: BU. 1945.

Name.	Builder.	Laid dwn.	Launched.	Completed.
HISHI.	Maizuru Navy yd.	Unknown.	Unknown.	Unknown.

Fate: BU. 1945.

Name.	Builder.	Laid dwn.	Launched.	Completed.
YAEZAKURA.	Yokosuka Navy yd.	Unknown.	Unknown.	Unknown.

Fate: BU incomplete. 1945.

Name.	Builder.	Laid dwn.	Launched.	Completed.
TOCHI.	Yokosuka Navy yd.	Unknown.	Unknown.	Unknown.

Fate: BU incomplete. 1945.

Name.	Builder.	Laid dwn.	Launched.	Completed.
YADAKE.	Yokosuka Navy yd.	Unknown.	Unknown.	Unknown.

Fate: BU incomplete.

Name.	Builder.	Laid dwn.	Launched.	Completed.
KATSURA.	Fujinagata Osaka.	Unknown.	Unknown.	Unknown.

Fate: BU incomplete. 1945.

TORPEDO BOATS.

TOMOZURU (Class).

Displacement: 737 Tonnes. Compliment: 113.

Dimensions:	269'0" x 24'3" x 8'2".
Machinery:	2 Boilers, 2 Shaft geared turbines. 11,000Shp = 30.0Kts.
Fuel Cap:	Oil. 150 Tons..
Armour:	None.
Armament:	3 x 5.0", 10 x 25mmAA, 1 x 40mm AA, 4 x 21"TT, 48 DC.

Name.	Builder.	Laid dwn.	Launched.	Completed.
TOMOZURU.	Maizuru Navy yd.	Unknown.	01-10-33.	Unknown.

Fate: sunk. 24-03-45. By US Navy A/c.

Name.	Builder.	Laid dwn.	Launched.	Completed.
MANAZURU.	Fujinagata Osaka.	Unknown.	11-07-33.	Unknown.

Fate: Sunk. 01-03-45. By US Navy A/c.

Name.	Builder.	Laid dwn.	Launched.	Completed.
CHIDORI.	Maizuru Navy yd.	Unknown.	01-04-33.	Unknown.

Fate: Sunk. 24-12-44. Torpedoed by US S/m.

Name.	Builder.	Laid dwn.	Launched.	Completed.
HATSUKARI.	Fujinagata Osaka.	Unknown.	19-12-33.	Unknown.

Fate: BU 1946.

OTORI (Class).

Displacement: 1,040 Tonnes. Compliment: 113.

Dimensions:	269'0" x 26'10" x 9'1".
Machinery:	2 Boilers. 2 Shaft geared turbines. 19,000Shp = 30.5Kts.
Fuel Cap:	Unknown.
Armour:	None.
Armament:	3 x 4.7", 11 x 25mmAA, 1 x 40mm AA, 3 x 21"TT, 48 DC.

Name.	Builder.	Laid dwn.	Launched.	Completed.
OTORI.	Maizuru Navy yd.	Unknown.	25-04-35.	Unknown.

Fate: Sunk. 12-06-44. By US Navy A/c.

Name.	Builder.	Laid dwn.	Launched.	Completed.
HAYABUSA.	Yokohama Co Yokohama.	Unknown.	28-10-35.	Unknown.

Fate: Sunk. 24-09-44. By US Navy A/c.

Name.	Builder.	Laid dwn.	Launched.	Completed.
HATO.	Ishikawjima Tokyo.	Unknown.	25-01-37.	Unknown.

Fate: Sunk. By US Navy A/c.

Name.	Builder.	Laid dwn.	Launched.	Completed.
KASASAGI.	Osaka Iron Wks Osaka.	Unknown.	28-10-35.	Unknown.

Fate: Sunk. 26-09-43. By US S/m.

TORPEDO BOATS. (Continued).

OTORI (Class). (Continued).

Name.	Builder.	Laid dwn.	Launched.	Completed.
HYODORI.	Ishikawajama Tokyo.	Unknown.	23-10-35.	Unknown.

Fate: Sunk. 17-11-44. By US S/m.

Name.	Builder.	Laid dwn.	Launched.	Completed.
SAGI.	Harima Co Harima.	Unknown.	30-01-37.	Unknown.

Fate: Sunk. 08-11-44. By US S/m.

Name.	Builder.	Laid dwn.	Launched.	Completed.
KARI.	Mitsibushi Yokohama.	Unknown.	20-01-37.	Unknown.

Fate: Sunk. 16-07-45. By US S/m.

Name.	Builder.	Laid dwn.	Launched.	Completed.
KIJI.	Tama Okayama.	Unknown.	26-01-37.	Unknown.

Fate: To USSR 1947.

SUBMARINES.

KD1 (Class).

Displacement: 1,500/2,500 Tonnes.   Compliment: 60.
Dimensions: 300'0" x 28'10" x 15'1".
Machinery: 4 Shaft Diesel/Electric Motors. 52Bhp/2,000Bhp = 20/10Kts.
Fuel Cap: Diesel, Unknown.
Armour: None.
Armament: 1 x 4.7", 1 x 3.0", 8 x 21"TT.

Number.	Builder.	Laid dwn.	Launched.	Completed.
I.51.(ex No 44)	Kure Navy yd.	Unknown.	29-11-21.	Unknown.

Fate: Sold 1941.

KD2 (Class).

Displacement: 1,500/2,500 Tonnes.   Compliment: 60.
Dimensions: 330'0" x 25'10" x 16'10".
Machinery: 2 Shaft Diesel/Electric Motors. 6,800Bhp/2000Bhp = 22/10Kts.
Fuel Cap: Diesel, Unknown.
Armour: None.
Armament: 1 x 4.7", 1 x 3.0", 8 x 21", TT.

Number.	Builder.	Laid dwn.	Launched.	Completed.
I.52.(Ex 51).	Kure Navy yd.	Unknown.	12-06-22.	Unknown.

Fate: BU 1948.

KD3a (Class).

Displacement: 1,800/2,300 Tonnes.   Compliment: 64.
Dimensions: 330'0" x 26'2" x 15'10".
Machinery: 2 Shaft Diesel/Electric Motors. 6,800Bhp/1800Bhp = 22/10Kts.
Fuel Cap: Diesel, Unknown.
Armour: None.
Armament: 1 x 4.7", 1 x 3.0", 8 x 21"TT.

Number.	Builder.	Laid dwn.	Launched.	Completed.
I.53.	Kure Navy yd.	Unknown.	05-08-25.	Unknown.

Fate: BU 1948.

Number.	Builder.	Laid dwn.	Launched.	Completed.
I.54.	Sasebo Navy yd.	Unknown.	15-03-26.	Unknown.

Fate: BU 1946.

Number.	Builder.	Laid dwn.	Launched.	Completed.
I.55.	Kure Navy yd.	Unknown.	02-09-25.	Unknown.

Fate: BU1946.

Number.	Builder.	Laid dwn.	Launched.	Completed.
I.58.	Yokohama Navy yd.	Unknown.	03-10-25.	Unknown.

Fate: Scuttled. 01-04-46.

SUBMARINES. (Continued).

KD3b (Class).
Displacement: 1,800/2,300 Tonnes. Compliment: 79.
Dimensions: 330'0" x 26'2" x 15'10".
Machinery: 2 Shaft Diesel/Electric Motors. 6,800Bhp/1,800Bhp = 22/10Kts.
Fuel Cap: Diesel, Unknown.
Armour: None.
Armament: 1 x 4.7", 1 x 3.0", 8 x 21"TT.

Number.	Builder.	Laid dwn.	Launched.	Completed.
I.56.	Kure Navy yd.	Unknown.	23-03-28.	Unknown.

Fate: Scuttled 01-04-46.

Number.	Builder.	Laid dwn.	Launched.	Completed.
I.57.	Kure Navy yd.	Unknown.	01-10-28.	Unknown.

Fate Scuttled 01-04-46.

Number.	Builder.	Laid dwn.	Launched.	Completed.
I.59.	Yokosuka Navy yd.	Unknown.	23-03-29.	Unknown.

Fate: Scuttled. 01-04-46.

Number.	Builder.	Laid dwn.	Launched.	Completed.
I.63.	Sasebo Navy yd.	Unknown.	28-09-27.	Unknown.

Fate: BU 1940.

Number.	Builder.	Laid dwn.	Launched.	Completed.
I.60.	Sasebo Navy yd.	Unknown.	24-04-29.	Unknown.

Fate: Sunk. By British destroyer. Java sea.

KD4 (Class).
Displacement: 1700/2300 Tonnes. Compliment: 58.
Dimensions: 320'6" x 25'7" x 15'10".
Machinery: 2 Shaft Diesel/Electric Motors. 6,000Bhp/1800Bhp = 20/8.5Kts.
Fuel Cap: Diesel, Unknown.
Armour: None.
Armament: 1 x 4.7", 6 x 21"TT.

Number.	Builder.	Laid dwn.	Launched.	Completed.
I.61.	Mitsibushi Kobe.	Unknown.	12-11-27.	Unknown.

Fate: Sunk. 06-10-41. Collision. Feb 1942 Salved & scrapped.

Number.	Builder.	Laid dwn.	Launched.	Completed.
I.62.	Mitsibushi Kobe.	Unknown.	29-11-28.	Unknown.

Fate: (Became Kaiten carrier). Scuttled 01-04-46.

Number.	Builder.	Laid dwn.	Launched.	Completed.
I.64.	Kure Navy yd.	Unknown.	05-10-29.	Unknown.

Fate: Sunk. 17-05-42. Torpedoed by US S/m TRITON.

SUBMARINES. (Continued).

KD5 (Class).
Displacement: 1,705/2,330 Tonnes.   Compliment: 70-82.
Dimensions: 320'6" x 26'11" x 15'5".
Machinery: 2 Shaft Diesel/Electric Motors. 6,000Bhp/1,800Bhp = 20.5/8.2Kts.
Fuel Cap: Diesel, Unknown.
Armour: None.
Armament: 1 x 3.9", 1 x 13.2mm AA. (Kaiten Carrier)

Number.	Builder.	Laid dwn.	Launched.	Completed.
I.65.	Kure Navy yd.	Unknown.	02-06-31.	Unknown.

Fate: Sunk. 27-06-45. While on a mission.

Number.	Builder.	Laid dwn.	Launched.	Completed.
I.66.	Sasebo Navy yd.	Unknown.	02-06-31.	Unknown.

Fate: Sunk. Torpedoed by HM S/m TELEMACHUS.

KD6a (Class).
Displacement: 1,785/2,440 Tonnes.   Compliment: 60-84.
Dimensions :   343'6" x 26'11" x 15'0".
Machinery: 2 Shaft Diesel/Electric Motors. 9,000Bhp/1,800Bhp = 23/8.2Kts.
Fuel Cap: Diesel, Unknown.
Armour: None.
Armament: 1 x 3.9", (I.71, 72, 73 1 x 4.7"). 1 x 13.2mm AA, 6 x 21"TT.

Number.	Builder.	Laid dwn.	Launched.	Completed.
I.68.	Kure Navy yd.	Unknown.	15-02-34.	Unknown.

Fate: Sunk. Cause unknown. Modified as transport.

Number.	Builder.	Laid dwn.	Launched.	Completed.
I.69.	Mitsibushi Kobe.	Unknown.	15-02-34.	Unknown.

Fate: Sunk. Cause unknown. Modified as transport.

Number.	Builder.	Laid dwn.	Launched.	Completed.
I.69.	Kure Navy yd.	Unknown.	15-02-34.	Unknown.

Fate: Sunk. 04-04-41. Cause unknown. Modified as Transport.

Number.	Builder.	Laid dwn.	Launched.	Completed.
I.70.	Sasebo Navy yd.	Unknown.	14-06-34.	Unknown.

Fate: Sunk. 10-12-41. During pearl Harbour cause unknown.

Number.	Builder.	Laid dwn.	Launched.	Completed.
I.71.	Kawasaki Kobe.	Unknown.	25-08-34.	Unknown.

Fate: Sunk. 01-02-44. Cause unknown.

Number.	Builder.	Laid dwn.	Launched.	Completed.
I.72.	Mitsibushi Kobe.	Unknown.	20-06-35.	Unknown.

Fate: Sunk. 10-11-42. Cause unknown.

SUBMARINES. (Continued).

KD6a. (Continued).

Number.	Builder.	Laid dwn.	Launched.	Completed.
I.73.	Kawasaki Kobe.	Unknown.	20-06-35.	Unknown.

Fate: Sunk. 27 01 42. In the Solomons & Central Pacific areas. Cause unknown.

KD6b (Class).

Displacement: 1,810/2,564 Tonnes.   Compliment: 60-84.
Dimensions: 344'6" x 26'11" x 15'1".
Machinery: 2 Shaft Diesel/Electric Motors. 9,000Bhp/1800Shp = 23/8.2Kts.
Fuel Cap: Diesel, Unknown.
Armour: None.
Armament: 1 x 4.7", 4 x 13.2mm AA, 6 x 21"TT.

Number.	Builder.	Laid dwn.	Launched.	Completed.
I.74.	Sasebo Navy yd.	Unknown.	28-03-37.	Unknown.

Renumbered I.174.
Fate: Sunk. 12-04-44. By US Forces Central Pacific.

Number.	Builder.	Laid dwn.	Launched.	Completed.
I.75.	Mitsibushi Kobe.	Unknown.	16-09-36.	Unknown.

Renumbered I.175.
Fate: Sunk. 04-02-44. By US Forces Central Pacific.

KD7 (Class).

Displacement: 1803/2602 Tonnes.   Compliment: 84.
Dimensions: 346'2" x 27'1" x 15'1".
Machinery: 2 Shaft Diesel/Electric Motors. 8,000Bhp/1800Bhp = 23.1/8Kts.
Fuel Cap: Diesel, Unknown.
Armour: None.
Armament: 1 x 4.7", 2 x 25mm AA, 6 x 21"TT.

Number.	Builder.	Laid dwn.	Launched.	Completed.
I.176. (Ex I.76).	Unknown.	Unknown.	07-06-41.	Unknown.

Fate: Modified as transport. Sunk. 16/17-05-44. Accident.

Number.	Builder.	Laid dwn.	Launched.	Completed.
I.177. (Ex I.77).	Unknown.	Unknown.	20-12-41.	Unknown.

Fate: Modified as transport. Sunk. 03-10-44. Accident.

Number.	Builder.	Laid dwn.	Launched.	Completed.
I.178. (Ex I.78).	Unknown.	Unknown.	24-02-42.	Unknown.

Fate: Modified as transport. Sunk. 14-07-42. Accident. Refloated, JMSDF for tests.

Number.	Builder.	Laid dwn.	Launched.	Completed.
I.179. (Ex I.79).	Unknown.	Unknown.	16-07-42.	Unknown.

Fate: Accident. Refloated 1957 by the JMSDF for tests.

SUBMARINES. (Continued).

KD7 (Class). (Continued).

Number.	Builder.	Laid dwn.	Launched.	Completed.
I.180. (Ex I.80).	Unknown.	Unknown.	07-02-42.	Unknown.

Fate: Sunk. 26-04-44. By US Forces S/W Pacific. Lack of official records dates are questionable.

Number.	Builder.	Laid dwn.	Launched.	Completed.
I.181. (Ex I.81).	Unknown.	Unknown.	02-05-42.	Unknown.

Fate: Sunk. 16-01-44. By US Forces S/W Pacific. Lack of official records dates are questionable.

Number.	Builder.	Laid dwn.	Launched.	Completed.
I.182. (Ex I.82).	Unknown.	Unknown.	30-05-42.	Unknown.

Fate: Sunk. 01-09-43. By US Forces S/W Pacific. Lack of official records dates are questionable.

Number.	Builder.	Laid dwn.	Launched.	Completed.
I.183. (Ex I.83).	Unknown.	Unknown.	21-01-43.	Unknown.

Fate: Sunk. 28/29-04-44. By US Forces S/W Pacific. Lack of official records dates are questionable.

Number.	Builder.	Laid dwn.	Launched.	Completed.
I.184. (Ex I.84).	Unknown.	Unknown.	12-12-42.	Unknown.

Fate: Sunk. 19-06-44. By US Forces S/W Pacific. Lack of official records dates are questionable.

Number.	Builder.	Laid dwn.	Launched.	Completed.
I.185. (Ex I.85).	Unknown.	Unknown.	16-09-43.	Unknown.

Fate: Sunk. 22-06-44. By US Forces S/W Pacific. Lack of official records dates are questionable.

J1 (Class).

Displacement. 2,135/2,791 Tonnes.   Compliment: 92.
Dimensions: 319'11" x 30'3" x 16'5".
Machinery: 2 Shaft Diesel/Electric Motors. 6,000Bhp/2,600Bhp = 18/8Kts.
Fuel Cap: Diesel, Unknown.
Armour: None.
Armament: 1 x 5.5", 6 x 21"TT.

Number.	Builder.	Laid dwn.	Launched.	Completed.
I.01. (Ex I.74.)	Kawasaki Kobe.	Unknown.	15-10-24.	Unknown.

Fate: Modified as transport. Sunk. 29-01-43. South west Pacific.

Number.	Builder.	Laid dwn.	Launched.	Completed.
I.02. (Ex I.75.)	Kawasaki Kobe.	Unknown.	23-02-25.	Unknown.

Fate: Modified as transport. Sunk. 07-04-43. South west Pacific.

SUBMARINES. (Continued).

J1. (Class). (Continued).

Number.	Builder.	Laid dwn.	Launched.	Completed.
I.03. (Ex I.76.)	Kawasaki Kobe.	Unknown.	08-06-25.	Unknown.

Fate: modified as transport. Sunk. 09/10 02-44. South west Pacific.

Number.	Builder.	Laid dwn.	Launched.	Completed.
I.02. (Ex I.75.)	Kawasaki Kobe.	Unknown.	22-05-28.	Unknown.

Fate: Modified as transport. Sunk. 25-12-42. South west Pacific.

J1-M (Class).
Displacement: 2,243/2,921 Tonnes.   Compliment: 93.
Dimensions: 319'11" x 29'9" x 16'2".
Machinery: 2 Shaft Diesel/Electric Motors. 6,000Bhp/2,600Bhp = 18/8Kts.
Fuel Cap: Diesel, Unknown.
Armour: None.
Armament: 1 x 5.5", 1 Aircraft. 6 x 21"TT.

Number.	Builder.	Laid dwn.	Launched.	Completed.
I.05.	Kawasaki Kobe.	Unknown.	19-06-31.	Unknown.

Fate: Sunk. US Navy. East of Guam.

J2. (Class).
Displacement: 2,243/3,061 Tonnes.   Compliment: 97.
Dimensions: 323'2" x 29'9" x 17'5".
Machinery: 2 Shaft Diesel/Electric Motors. 6,000Bhp/2600Bhp = 20/7.5Kts.
Fuel Cap: Diesel, Unknown.
Armour: None.
Armament: 1 x 5.5", 1 x 13.2mm AA. 1 Aircraft.

Number.	Builder.	Laid dwn.	Launched.	Completed.
I.06.	Kawasaki Kobe.	Unknown.	31-03-34.	Unknown.

Fate: Sunk. 14-07-44. US Forces. Saipan area.

J3. (Class).
Displacement. 2,525/3,538 Tonnes.   Compliment: 100.
Dimensions: 358'7" x 29'10" x 9'10".
Machinery: 2 Shaft Diesel/Electric Motors. 11,200Bhp/2,800Bhp = 23/8.0Kts.
Fuel Cap: Diesel, Unknown.
Armour: None.
Armament: 1 x 5.5", 1 x 13.2mm AA. 6 x 21"TT. 1 Aircraft.

Number.	Builder.	Laid dwn.	Launched.	Completed.
I.07.	Kure Navy yd.	Unknown.	03-07-35.	Unknown.

Fate: Converted to Kaiten carrier. Sunk. 22-06-43. US Forces. The Alutians.

SUBMARINES. (Continued).

J.3. (Class). (Continued).

Number.	Builder.	Laid dwn.	Launched.	Completed.
I.08.	Kawasaki Kobe.	Unknown	20-07-36.	Unknown

Fate: Converted to Kaiten carrier. Sunk. 31-05-45. US Forces. Near Okinawa.

KRS. (Class).

Displacement: 1,383/1,768 Tonnes. Compliment: 51-70.
Dimensions: 297'6" x 24'8" x 14'6".
Machinery: 2 Shaft Diesel/Electric Motors. 2400Bhp/1100Bhp = 15/5.0Kts.
Fuel Cap: Diesel, Unknown.
Armour: None.
Armament: 1 x 5.5", Mines 42, 6 x 21"TT.

Number.	Builder.	Laid dwn.	Launched.	Completed.
I.121.(Ex I.21/48.)	Kawasaki Kobe.	Unknown.	30-03-26.	Unknown.

Fate: BU. 1946.

Number.	Builder.	Laid dwn.	Launched.	Completed.
I.122.(Ex I.22/49).	Kawasaki Kobe.	Unknown.	08-11-26.	Unknown.

Fate: Used for training from 1943. Sunk. 10-06-45. Torpedoed by USS/m SKATE.

Number.	Builder.	Laid dwn.	Launched.	Completed.
I.123.(Ex I.23/50).	Kawasaki Kobe.	Unknown.	19-03-27.	Unknown.

Fate: Sunk. 29-08-42. Off Guadacanal.

Number.	Builder.	Laid dwn.	Launched.	Completed.
I.124.(Ex I.24).	Kawasaki Kobe.	Unknown.	12-12-27.	Unknown.

Fate: Sunk. 20-01-42. In the East Indies.
N.B. All were modified to refuel 'reconn' Sea-planes.

A1. (Class).

Displacement: 2,919/4,149 Tonnes. Compliment: 114.
Dimensions: 373'0" x 31'4" x 17'7".
Machinery: 2 Shaft Diesel/Electric Motors. 12,400Bhp/2,400Bhp = 23.5/8.0Kts.
Fuel Cap: Diesel, Unknown.
Armour: None.
Armament: 1 x 5.5", 2 x 25mm AA, 6 x 21"TT, 1 Aircraft.

Number.	Builder.	Laid dwn.	Launched.	Completed.
I.9.	Kure Navy yd.	Unknown.	29-05-39.	Unknown.

Fate: Sunk. 11/15-06-43. US Forces in the Alutians.

Number.	Builder.	Laid dwn.	Launched.	Completed.
I.10.	Kawasaki Kobe.	Unknown	20-09-39.	Unknown.

Fate: Sunk. 04-07-44. US Forces. Nr Saipan.

SUBMARINES. (Continued).

A1. (Class). (Continued).

Number.	Builder.	Laid dwn.	Launched.	Completed.
I.11.	Kawasaki Kobe.	Unknown.	28-02-41.	Unknown.

Fate: Sunk. After 11-01-44. US Forces. Nr Samoa.

A2. (Class).

Displacement: 2,934/4,172 Tonnes.　　　　　　Compliment: 114.
Dimensions:　　373'0" x 31'4" x 17'8".
Machinery:　　2 Shaft Diesel/Electric Motors. 4,700Bhp/1,200Shp = 17.5/6.2Kts.
Fuel Cap:　　Diesel, Unknown.
Armour:　　None.
Armament:　　1 x 5.5", 2 x 25mm AA, 6 x 21" TT, 1 Aircraft.

Number.	Builder.	Laid dwn.	Launched.	Completed.
I.12.	Kawasaki Kobe.	Unknown.	1943.	Unknown.

Fate: Sunk. After 05-01-45. Cause unknown.

AM. (Class).

Displacement: 3,603/4,762 Tonnes.　　　　　　Compliment: 114.
Dimensions:　　373'0" x 38.5" x 19'4".
Machinery:　　2 Shaft Diesel/Electric Motors. 4,400Bhp/600Shp = 16.7/5.5Kts.
Fuel Cap:　　Diesel, Unknown.
Armour:　　None.
Armament:　　1 x 5.5", 7 x 25mm AA, 6 x 21"TT, 2 Aircraft.

Number.	Builder.	Laid dwn.	Launched.	Completed.
I.13.	Kawasaki Kobe.	Unknown.	1944.	Unknown.

Fate: Sunk. 16-07-45. US Forces. Coast of Japan.

Number.	Builder.	Laid dwn.	Launched.	Completed.
I.14.	Kawasaki Kobe.	Unknown.	1944.	Unfinished.

Fate: BU. 1946.

Number.	Builder.	Laid dwn.	Launched.	Completed.
I.15.	Kawasaki Kobe.	Unknown.	12-04-44.	Unfinished.

Fate: BU. 1945.

Number.	Builder.	Laid dwn.	Launched.	Completed.
I.16.	Kawasaki Kobe.	Unknown.	10-06-44.	Unfinished.

Fate: BU. 1947.

SUBMARINES. (Continued).

B1. (Class)
Displacement: 2,589/3,654 Tonnes.   Compliment: 101.
Dimensions: 356'7" x 30.6" x 16'10".
Machinery: 2 Shaft Diesel/Electric Motors. 12,400Bhp/2,000Bhp = 23.6/8.0Kts.
Fuel Cap: Diesel, Unknown.
Armour: None.
Armament: 1 x 5.5", 2 x 25mm AA, 6 x 21"TT, 1 Aircraft.

Number.	Builder.	Laid dwn.	Launched.	Completed.
I.15.	Kure Navy yd.	Unknown.	07-03-39.	Unknown.

Fate: Sunk. 10-11-42. US Forces.

Number.	Builder.	Laid dwn.	Launched.	Completed.
I.17.	Yokosuka Navy yd.	Unknown.	19-07-39.	Unknown.

Fate: Sunk. 29-11/03-12-43. US Forces. Central Pacific & Phillipines.

Number.	Builder.	Laid dwn.	Launched.	Completed.
I.19.	Mitsibushi Kobe.	Unknown.	16-09-39.	Unknown.

Fate: Sunk. 25-11-43. By US Forces.

Number.	Builder.	Laid dwn.	Launched.	Completed.
I.21.	Kawasaki Kobe.	Unknown.	24-02-40.	Unknown.

Fate: Sunk. 27/29-11-43. By US Forces.

Number.	Builder.	Laid dwn.	Launched.	Completed.
I.23.	Yokosuka Navy yd.	Unknown.	24-11-39.	Unknown.

Fate: Sunk. 26-02-42. By US Forces.

Number.	Builder.	Laid dwn.	Launched.	Completed.
I.25.	Mitsibushi Kobe.	Unknown.	08-06-40.	Unknown.

Fate: Sunk. 03/05-09-43. By US Forces.

Number.	Builder.	Laid dwn.	Launched.	Completed.
I.26.	Kure Navy yd.	Unknown.	10-04-40.	Unknown.

Fate: Sunk. 24-10-44. By US Forces.

Number.	Builder.	Laid dwn.	Launched.	Completed.
I.27.	Sasebo Navy yd.	Unknown.	06-06-40.	Unknown.

Fate: Sunk. 12-02-44. Torpedoed by HMS/m TAURUS off Penang.

Number.	Builder.	Laid dwn.	Launched.	Completed.
I.28.	Mitsibushi Kobe.	Unknown.	18-12-40.	Unknown.

Fate: Sunk. 17-05-42. By US Forces.

Number.	Builder.	Laid dwn.	Launched.	Completed.
I.29.	Yokosuka Navy yd.	Unknown.	29-09-40.	Unknown.

Fate: Sunk. 26-07-44. By US Forces.

Number.	Builder.	Laid dwn.	Launched.	Completed.
I.30.	Kure Navy yd.	Unknown.	17-09-40.	Unknown.

Fate: Sunk. 13-10-42. By US Forces.

SUBMARINES. (Continued).

B1 (Class). (Continued).

Number.	Builder.	Laid dwn.	Launched.	Completed.
I.31.	Yokosuka Navy yd.	Unknown.	13-03-41.	Unknown.

Fate: Sunk. 13-06-44. By US Forces.

Number.	Builder.	Laid dwn.	Launched.	Completed.
I.32.	Sasebo Navy yd.	Unknown.	17-12-40.	Unknown.

Fate: Sunk. 24-03-44. By US Forces.

Number.	Builder.	Laid dwn.	Launched.	Completed.
I.33.	Mitsibushi Kobe.	Unknown.	01-05-41.	Unknown.

Fate: Sunk. 13-06-44. By US Forces.

Number.	Builder.	Laid dwn.	Launched.	Completed.
I.34.	Sasebo Navy yd.	Unknown.	29-09-41.	Unknown.

Fate: Sunk. 13-11-43. By British Destroyers near ADDU ATOLL.

Number.	Builder.	Laid dwn.	Launched.	Completed.
I.35.	Mitsibushi Kobe.	Unknown.	24-09-41.	Unknown.

Fate: Sunk. 22-11-43. By US Forces.

Number.	Builder.	Laid dwn.	Launched.	Completed.
I.36.	Yokosuka Navy yd.	Unknown.	01-11-41.	Unknown.

Fate: Scuttled. 01-04-46.

Number.	Builder.	Laid dwn.	Launched.	Completed.
I.37.	Kure Navy yd.	Unknown.	27-10-44.	Unknown.

Fate: Sunk. 19-11-44. By US Forces.

Number.	Builder.	Laid dwn.	Launched.	Completed.
I.38.	Sasebo Navy yd.	Unknown.	15-04-42.	Unknown.

Fate: Sunk. 12-11-44. By US Forces.

Number.	Builder.	Laid dwn.	Launched.	Completed.
I.39.	Sasebo Navy yd.	Unknown.	15-04-42.	Unknown.

Fate: Sunk. 26-11-43. By US Forces.

B2. (Class).

Displacement: 2,624/3,700 Tonnes.   Compliment: 101.
Dimensions: 356'7" x 30.6" x 17'1".
Machinery: 2 Shaft Diesel/Electric Motors. 11,000Bhp/2,000Bhp = 23.5Kts.
Fuel Cap: Diesel, Unknown.
Armour: None.
Armament: 1 x 5.5", 2 x 25mm AA, 6 x 21" TT, 1 Aircraft.

Number.	Builder.	Laid dwn.	Launched.	Completed.
I.40.	Kure Navy yd.	Unknown.	1942.	Unknown.

Fate: Sunk. 29-11/03-12-43. US Forces. Central Pacific & Phillipines.

SUBMARINES. (Continued).

B2. (Class). (Continued).

Number.	Builder.	Laid dwn.	Launched.	Completed.
I.41.	Kure Navy yd.	Unknown.	1943.	Unknown.

Fate: Sunk. 28-11-44. US Forces. Central Pacific & Phillipines.

Number.	Builder.	Laid dwn.	Launched.	Completed.
I.42.	Kure Navy yd.	Unknown.	1943.	Unknown.

Fate: Sunk. 23-03-44. US Forces. Central Pacific & Phillipines.

Number.	Builder.	Laid dwn.	Launched.	Completed.
I.43.	Sasebo Navy yd.	Unknown.	1943.	Unknown.

Fate: Sunk. 15-02-44. US Forces. Central Pacific & Phillipines.

Number.	Builder.	Laid dwn.	Launched.	Completed.
I.44.	Yokosuka Navy yd.	Unknown.	1943.	Unknown.

Fate: Sunk. 29-04-45. US Forces. Central Pacific & Phillipines.

Number.	Builder.	Laid dwn.	Launched.	Completed.
I.45.	Sasebo Navy yd.	Unknown.	1943.	Unknown.

Fate: Sunk. 28-10-44. US Forces. Central Pacific & Phillipines.

B3. (Class).

Displacement. 2,607/3,688 Tonnes.   Compliment: 101.
Dimensions: 356'7" x 30.6" x 17'0".
Machinery: 2 Shaft Diesel/Electric Motors. 47,000Bhp/1,200Bhp = 17.7/6.5Kts.
Fuel Cap: Diesel, Unknown.
Armour: None.
Armament: 1 x 5.5", 2 x 25mm AA, 6 x 21"TT, 1 Aircraft.

Number.	Builder.	Laid dwn.	Launched.	Completed.
I.54.	Yokosuka Navy yd.	Unknown.	1943.	Unknown.

Fate: Sunk. 28-10-44. Cause unknown.

Number.	Builder.	Laid dwn.	Launched.	Completed.
I.56.	Yokosuka Navy yd.	Unknown.	1943.	Unknown.

Fate: Sunk. 18-04-45. Cause unknown.

Number.	Builder.	Laid dwn.	Launched.	Completed.
I.58.	Yokosuka Navy yd.	Unknown.	1944.	Unknown.

Fate: Sunk US Cruiser Indianapolis. Scuttled. 01-04-06.

SUBMARINES. (Continued).

C1. (Class).
Displacement. 2,554/3,561 Tonnes.   Compliment: 101.
Dimensions: 358'7" x 29.10" x 17'7".
Machinery: 2 Shaft Diesel/Electric Motors. 12,100Bhp/12,00Bhp = 23.6/8.0Kts.
Fuel Cap: Diesel, Unknown.
Armour: None.
Armament: 1 x 5.5", 2 x 25mm AA, 8 x 21"TT.

Number.	Builder.	Laid dwn.	Launched.	Completed.
I.16.	Mitsibushi Kobe.	Unknown.	28-07-38.	Unknown.

Fate: Sunk. 19-05-44. Destroyer. US. ENGLAND.

Number.	Builder.	Laid dwn.	Launched.	Completed.
I.19.	Sasebo Navy yd.	Unknown.	12-11-38.	Unknown.

Fate: Sunk. 11-02-43. US Forces in the Pacific.

Number.	Builder.	Laid dwn.	Launched.	Completed.
I.20.	Mitsibushi Kobe.	Unknown.	25-01-39.	Unknown.

Fate: Sunk. 03-09-43. US Forces in the Pacific.

Number.	Builder.	Laid dwn.	Launched.	Completed.
I.22.	Kawasaki Kobe.	Unknown.	23-12-38.	Unknown.

Fate: Sunk. 05-10/04-11-42. US Forces in the Pacific.

Number.	Builder.	Laid dwn.	Launched.	Completed.
I.24.	Sasebo Navy yd.	Unknown.	12-11-39.	Unknown.

Fate: Sunk. 10/11-06-43. US Forces in the Pacific.

C2. (Class).
Displacement. 2,557/3,564 Tonnes.   Compliment: 101.
Dimensions: 358'7" x 29.10" x 17'7".
Machinery: 2 Shaft Diesel/Electric Motors. 11,000Bhp/2,000Bhp = Kts.
Fuel Cap: Diesel, Unknown.
Armour: None.
Armament: 1 x 5.5", 2 x 25mm AA, 8 x 21" TT.

Number.	Builder.	Laid dwn.	Launched.	Completed.
I.46.	Sasebo Navy yd.	Unknown.	1943.	Unknown.

Fate: Sunk. 10/11-06-43.

Number.	Builder.	Laid dwn.	Launched.	Completed.
I.47.	Sasebo Navy yd.	Unknown.	1943.	Unknown.

Fate: Scuttled. 01-04-46.

Number.	Builder.	Laid dwn.	Launched.	Completed.
I.48.	Sasebo Navy yd.	Unknown.	Unknown.	Unknown.

Fate: Sunk. 23-06-45. Cause unknown.

SUBMARINES. (Continued).

C3. (Class).
Displacement. 2,564/3,544 Tonnes.   Compliment: 101.
Dimensions: 356'7" x 30.6" x 16'10".
Machinery: 2 Shaft Diesel/Electric Motors. 47,000Bhp/12,000Bhp = 17.7/6.5Kts.
Fuel Cap: Diesel, Unknown.
Armour: None.
Armament: 1 x 5.5", 2 x 25mm AA, 8 x 21"TT.

Number.	Builder.	Laid dwn.	Launched.	Completed.
I.52.	Kure Navy yd.	Unknown.	1943.	Unknown.

Fate: Sunk. 24-06-44. US Forces.

Number.	Builder.	Laid dwn.	Launched.	Completed.
I.53.	Kure Navy yd.	Unknown.	1943.	Unknown.

Fate: Scuttled. 01-04-46.

Number.	Builder.	Laid dwn.	Launched.	Completed.
I.55.	Kure Navy yd.	Unknown.	1943.	Unknown.

Fate: Sunk. 28-07-44. US Forces.

ST. (Class).
Displacement. 1,291/1,450 Tonnes.   Compliment: 31.
Dimensions: 259'2" x 19.0" x 17'11".
Machinery: 2 Shaft Diesel/Electric Motors. 2,750Bhp/5,000Shp = 17.7/6.5Kts.
Fuel Cap: Diesel, Unknown.
Armour: None.
Armament: 2 x 25mm AA, 4 x 21"TT.

Number.	Builder.	Laid dwn.	Launched.	Completed.
I.201.	Kure Navy yd.	Unknown.	1944.	Unknown.

Fate: To USA. 1945.

Number.	Builder.	Laid dwn.	Launched.	Completed.
I.202.	Kure Navy yd.	Unknown.	1944.	Unfinished.

Fate: Scuttled. 1946.

Number.	Builder.	Laid dwn.	Launched.	Completed.
I.203.	Kure Navy yd.	Unknown.	1944.	Unknown.

Fate: To USA. 1945.

Number.	Builder.	Laid dwn.	Launched.	Completed.
I.204.	Kure Navy yd.	Unknown.	16-12-44.	Unfinished.

Fate: Sunk. 22-06-45. Incomplete.

Number.	Builder.	Laid dwn.	Launched.	Completed.
I.205.	Kure Navy yd.	Unknown.	15-02-45.	Unfinished.

Fate: BU. Incomplete. 1948.

SUBMARINES. (Continued)

ST. (Class). (Continued).

Number.	Builder.	Laid dwn.	Launched.	Completed.
I.206	Kure Navy yd.	Unknown.	26 03 45.	Unfinished.

Fate: BU. Incomplete. 1946.

NB:- Experimental boats with increased battery capactiance.

SH. (Class).

Displacement. 3,512/4,290 Tonnes.   Compliment: 90.
Dimensions: 364'2" x 33.4" x 10'15".
Machinery: 2 Shaft Diesel/Electric Motors. 3,700Bhp/1,200Bhp = 15.8/6.3Kts.
Fuel Cap: Diesel, Unknown.
Armour: None.
Armament: 2 x 3" Trench Mortars, 7 x 25mm AA, 4 x 21"TT.

Number.	Builder.	Laid dwn.	Launched.	Completed.
I.351.	Kure Navy yd.	Unknown.	1944.	Unknown.

Fate: Sunk. 14-07-45. US S/m. East Indies.

Number.	Builder.	Laid dwn.	Launched.	Completed.
I.352.	Kure Navy yd.	Unknown.	23-04-44.	Unfinished.

Fate: Sunk. 22-06-45. US Aircraft.

D1. (Class).

Displacement. 1,779/2,215 Tonnes.   Compliment: 60.
Dimensions: 241'2" x 29.2" x 15'7".
Machinery: 2 Shaft Diesel/Electric Motors. 1,850Bhp/1,200Bhp = 13.0/6.5Kts.
Fuel Cap: Diesel, Unknown.
Armour: None.
Armament: 1 x 5.5, 2 x 25mm AA.
NB:- Converted to transports.

Number.	Builder.	Laid dwn.	Launched.	Completed.
I.361.	Kure Navy yd.	Unknown.	1943.	Unknown.

Fate: Sunk. 30-05-45. US Forces. Pacific.

Number.	Builder.	Laid dwn.	Launched.	Completed.
I.362.	Mitsibushi Kobe.	Unknown.	1943.	Unknown.

Fate: Sunk. 13/18-01-45. US Forces. Pacific.

Number.	Builder.	Laid dwn.	Launched.	Completed.
I.364.	Mitsibushi Kobe.	Unknown.	1943.	Unknown.

Fate: Sunk. 15/16-09-44. US Forces. Pacific.

Number.	Builder.	Laid dwn.	Launched.	Completed.
I.365.	Yokosuka Navy yd.	Unknown.	1944.	Unknown.

Fate: Fate: Sunk. 13/18-01-45. US Forces. Pacific.

SUBMARINES. (Continued).

D1. (Class). (Continued).

Number.	Builder.	Laid dwn.	Launched.	Completed.
I.368.	Yokosuka Navy yd.	Unknown.	1944.	Unknown.

Fate: Sunk. 27-02-45. US Forces. Pacific.

Number.	Builder.	Laid dwn.	Launched.	Completed.
I.370.	Mitsibushi Kobe.	Unknown.	1944.	Unknown.

Fate: Sunk. 26-02-45. US Forces. Pacific.

Number.	Builder.	Laid dwn.	Launched.	Completed.
I.371.	Mitsibushi Kobe.	Unknown.	1944.	Unknown.

Fate: Sunk. 24-02-45. US Forces. Pacific.

Number.	Builder.	Laid dwn.	Launched.	Completed.
I.372.	Yokosuka Navy yd.	Unknown.	1944.	Unknown.

Fate: US Forces. Pacific.

Number.	Builder.	Laid dwn.	Launched.	Completed.
I.363.	Kure Navy yd.	Unknown.	1943.	Unknown.

Fate: Sunk. 29-10-45. Mined. Post-war.

D2. (Class).

Displacement. 1,926/2,240 Tonnes.   Compliment: 60.
Dimensions: 242'9" x 29.2" x 16'7".
Machinery: 2 Shaft Diesel/Electric Motors. 1,750Bhp/1,200Bhp = 13.0/6.5Kts.
Fuel Cap: Diesel, Unknown.
Armour: None.
Armament: 1 x 5.5, 2 x 25mm AA.

Number.	Builder.	Laid dwn.	Launched.	Completed.
I.373.	Yokosuka Navy yd.	Unknown.	1944.	Unknown.

Fate: Sunk. 14-08-45. By US S/m SPIKEFISH.

Number.	Builder.	Laid dwn.	Launched.	Completed.
I.374.	Yokosuka Navy yd.	Unknown.	None.	Unfinished.

Fate: BU. Incomplete. 1945

STO. (Class).

Displacement. 5,223/6,560 Tonnes.   Compliment: 144.
Dimensions: 400'3" x 39.4" x 23'0".
Machinery: 2 Shaft Diesel/Electric Motors. 7,700Bhp/2,400Bhp = 18.7/6.5Kts.
Fuel Cap: Diesel, Unknown.
Armour: None.
Armament: 1 x 5.5, 10 x 25mm AA, 8 x 21"TT, 3 Aircraft.

Number.	Builder.	Laid dwn.	Launched.	Completed.
I.400.	Kure Navy yd.	Unknown.	1944.	Unknown.

Fate: Scuttled. 1946.

SUBMARINES. (Continued).

STO. (Class).

Number.	Builder.	Laid dwn.	Launched.	Completed.
I.401.	Sasebo Navy yd.	Unknown.	1944.	Unknown.

Fate: Scuttled. 1946.

Number.	Builder.	Laid dwn.	Launched.	Completed.
I.402.	Sasebo Navy yd.	Unknown.	1944.	Unknown.

Fate: Scuttled. 1946.

Number.	Builder.	Laid dwn.	Launched.	Completed.
I.404.	Kure Navy yd.	Unknown.	07-07-44.	Unfinished.

Fate: Sunk.28-07-45. Incomplete.

Number.	Builder.	Laid dwn.	Launched.	Completed.
I.405.	Kawasaki Kobe.	Unknown.	None.	Unfinished.

Fate: BU. Incomplete. 1945.

L4. (Class).

Displacement. 996/1,322 Tonnes.   Compliment: 47/60.
Dimensions: 250'3" x 24'3" x 12'4".
Machinery: 2 Shaft Diesel/Electric Motors. 2,400Bhp/1,600Shp = 16.5/9.0Kts.
Fuel Cap: Diesel, Unknown.
Armour: None.
Armament: 1 x 3.0, 1 x MG AA, 6 x 21"TT.

Number.	Builder.	Laid dwn.	Launched.	Completed.
RO.60. (Ex I.59).	Mitsibushi Kobe.	Unknown.	22-12-22.	Unknown.

Fate: Lost. 29-12-41. Wrecked on Kwajalein.

Number.	Builder.	Laid dwn.	Launched.	Completed.
RO.62. (Ex I.73).	Mitsibushi Kobe.	Unknown.	19-09-23.	Unknown.

Fate: BU. 1946.

Number.	Builder.	Laid dwn.	Launched.	Completed.
RO.63.	Mitsibushi Kobe.	Unknown.	25-10-26.	Unknown.

Fate: Sunk. 17-12-41. After collision with RO.62.

Number.	Builder.	Laid dwn.	Launched.	Completed.
RO.61.	Mitsibushi Kobe.	Unknown.	19-05-23.	Unknown.

Fate: Sunk. 31-08-42. By US Forces.

Number.	Builder.	Laid dwn.	Launched.	Completed.
RO.64.	Mitsibushi Kobe.	Unknown.	19-08-24.	Unknown.

Fate: Sunk. 12-04-45. By US Forces.

Number.	Builder.	Laid dwn.	Launched.	Completed.
RO.65.	Mitsibushi Kobe.	Unknown.	25-09-25.	Unknown.

Fate: Sunk. 04-11-42. By US Forces.

SUBMARINES. (Continued).

L4. (Class). (Continued).

Number.	Builder.	Laid dwn.	Launched.	Completed.
RO.66.	Mitsibushi Kobe.	Unknown.	25-10-26.	Unknown.

Fate: Sunk. 17-12-41. By US Forces.

Number.	Builder.	Laid dwn.	Launched.	Completed.
RO.67.	Mitsibushi Kobe.	Unknown.	18-03-26.	Unknown.

Fate: BU. 1946.

Number.	Builder.	Laid dwn.	Launched.	Completed.
RO.68.	Mitsibushi Kobe.	Unknown.	23-02-25.	Unknown.

Fate: No further knowledge.

K5. (Class).

Displacement. 940/1,042 Tonnes.   Compliment: 42.
Dimensions: 248'4" x 22'0" x 12'11".
Machinery: 2 Shaft Diesel/Electric Motors. 2,900Bhp/1,200Bhp = 19'0/8.2Kts.
Fuel Cap: Diesel, Unknown.
Armour: None.
Armament: 1 x 3.0, 1 x 13.2mm AA, 4 x 21"TT.

Number.	Builder.	Laid dwn.	Launched.	Completed.
RO.35.	Kure Navy yd.	Unknown.	10-10-34.	Unknown.

Fate: Sunk. 29-08-42. By RAAN Destroyer near Port Moresby.

Number.	Builder.	Laid dwn.	Launched.	Completed.
RO.34.	Mitsibushi Kobe.	Unknown.	12-12-35.	Unknown.

Fate: Sunk. 05-04-43. By US Destroyer. In the Solomans.

K6. (Class).

Displacement. 1,115/1,447 Tonnes.   Compliment: 54.
Dimensions: 264'1" x 23'2" x 13'4".
Machinery: 2 Shaft Diesels/Electric Motors. 4,200Bhp/1,200Shp = 19'7/8.0Kts.
Fuel Cap: Diesel, Unknown.
Armour: None.
Armament: 1 x 3.0, 2 x 25mm AA, 4 x 21" TT.

Number.	Builder.	Laid dwn.	Launched.	Completed.
R0.35.	Mitsibushi Kobe.	Unknown.	04-06-42.	Unknown.

Fate: Sunk. 25-08-43. Cause unknown.

Number.	Builder.	Laid dwn.	Launched.	Completed.
RO.36.	Mitsibushi Kobe.	Unknown.	14-10-42.	Unknown.

Fate: Sunk. 13-06-44. Cause unknown.

Number.	Builder.	Laid dwn.	Launched.	Completed.
RO.37.	Mitsibushi Kobe.	Unknown.	30-06-44.	Unknown.

Fate: Sunk. 22-01-44. Cause unknown

SUBMARINES. (Continued).

K6. (Class). (Continued).

Number.	Builder.	Laid dwn.	Launched.	Completed.
RO.38.	Mitsibushi Kobe.	Unknown.	24-12-42.	Unknown.

Fate: Sunk. 19/23 11-42. Cause unknown.

Number.	Builder.	Laid dwn.	Launched.	Completed.
RO.39.	Sasebo Navy yd.	Unknown.	06-03-43.	Unknown.

Fate: Sunk. 02-02-43. Cause unknown.

Number.	Builder.	Laid dwn.	Launched.	Completed.
RO.40.	Mitsibushi Kobe.	Unknown.	06-03-43.	Unknown.

Fate: Sunk. 02-02-44.

Number.	Builder.	Laid dwn.	Launched.	Completed.
RO.41.	Mitsibushi Kobe.	Unknown.	05-05-43.	Unknown.

Fate: Sunk. 23-02-43. Cause unknown.

Number.	Builder.	Laid dwn.	Launched.	Completed.
RO.42.	Sasebo Navy yd.	Unknown.	25-10-42.	Unknown.

Fate: Sunk. 10/11-06-43. Cause unknown.

Number.	Builder.	Laid dwn.	Launched.	Completed.
RO.44.	Tamano Tomano.	Unknown.	1943.	Unknown.

Fate: Sunk. 16-06-43.

Number.	Builder.	Laid dwn.	Launched.	Completed.
RO45.	Mitsibushi Kobe.	Unknown.	1943.	Unknown.

Fate: Sunk. 30-04-44. Cause unknown.

Number.	Builder.	Laid dwn.	Launched.	Completed.
RO.46.	Mitsibushi Kobe.	Unknown.	1943.	Unknown.

Fate: Sunk. 25-04-45. Cause unknown.

Number.	Builder.	Laid dwn.	Launched.	Completed.
RO.47.	Tamano Tomano.	Unknown.	1943.	Unknown.

Fate: Sunk. 05-04-45.

Number.	Builder.	Laid dwn.	Launched.	Completed.
RO.48.	Mitsibushi Kobe.	Unknown.	1943.	Unknown.

Fate: Sunk. 14-07-44. Cause unknown.

Number.	Builder.	Laid dwn.	Launched.	Completed.
RO.55.	Tamano Tomano.	Unknown	1944.	Unknown.

Fate: Sunk. 07-02-45. Cause unknown.

Number.	Builder.	Laid dwn.	Launched.	Completed.
RO.56.	Tamano Tomano.	Unknown.	1944.	Unknown.

Fate: Sunk. 09-04-45. Cause unknown.

SUBMARINES. (Continued).

KS. (Class).

Displacement. 601/782 Tonnes.		Compliment: 38.
Dimensions:	190'10" x 19'8" x 11'6".	
Machinery:	2 Shaft Diesel/Electric Motors. 1,100Bhp/760Bhp = 19'7/8.0Kts.	
Fuel Cap:	Diesel, Unknown.	
Armour:	None.	
Armament:	2 x 25mm AA, 4 x 21"TT	

Number.	Builder.	Laid dwn.	Launched.	Completed.
RO.100.	Kure Navy yd.	Unknown.	06-12-41.	Unknown.

Fate: Sunk. 25-11-43. By US Forces in the Pacific.

Number.	Builder.	Laid dwn.	Launched.	Completed.
RO.101.	Kawasaki Kobe.	Unknown.	17-05-42.	Unknown.

Fate: Sunk. 14-05-43. By US Forces in the Pacific.

Number.	Builder.	Laid dwn.	Launched.	Completed.
RO.102.	Kawasaki Kobe.	Unknown.	17-05-42.	Unknown.

Fate: Sunk. 14-04-43. By US Forces in the Pacific.

Number.	Builder.	Laid dwn.	Launched.	Completed.
RO.103.	Kure Navy yd.	Unknown.	06-12-41.	Unknown.

Fate: Sunk. 28/30-07-43. By US Forces in the Pacific.

Number.	Builder.	Laid dwn.	Launched.	Completed.
RO.104.	Kawasaki Kobe.	Unknown.	11-07-42.	Unknown.

Fate: Sunk. 23-05-42. By US Forces in the Pacific.

Number.	Builder.	Laid dwn.	Launched.	Completed.
RO.105.	Kawasaki Kobe.	Unknown.	11-07-42.	Unknown.

Fate: Sunk.31-05-44. By US Forces in the Pacific.

Number.	Builder.	Laid dwn.	Launched.	Completed.
RO.106.	Kure Navy yd.	Unknown.	30-05-42.	Unknown.

Fate: Sunk. 30-05-42. By US Forces in the Pacific.

Number.	Builder.	Laid dwn.	Launched.	Completed.
RO.107.	Kure Navy yd.	Unknown.	30-05-42.	

Fate: Sunk. 30-05-42. By US Forces in the Pacific.

Number.	Builder.	Laid dwn.	Launched.	Completed.
RO.108.	Kawasaki Kobe.	Unknown.	26-10-42.	Unknown.

Fate: Sunk. 26-05-44. By US Forces in the Pacific.

Number.	Builder.	Laid dwn.	Launched.	Completed.
RO.109.	Kawasaki Kobe.	Unknown.	1942.	Unknown.

Fate: Sunk. 29-04-45. By US Forces in the Pacific.

Number.	Builder.	Laid dwn.	Launched.	Completed.
RO.110.	Kawasaki Kobe.	Unknown.	1943.	Unknown.

Fate: Sunk. 11-02-44. By US Forces in the Pacific.

SUBMARINES. (Continued).

KS. (Class). (Continued).

Number.	Builder.	Laid dwn.	Launched.	Completed.
RO.111.	Kawasaki Kobe.	Unknown.	1943.	Unknown.

Fate: Sunk. 10-06-44. By US Forces in the Pacific.

Number.	Builder.	Laid dwn.	Launched.	Completed.
RO.112.	Kawasaki Kobe.	Unknown.	1943.	Unknown.

Fate: Sunk. By US Forces in the Pacific.

Number.	Builder.	Laid dwn.	Launched.	Completed.
RO.113.	Kawasaki Kobe.	Unknown.	1943.	Unknown.

Fate: Sunk. 12-02-45. By US Forces in the Pacific.

Number.	Builder.	Laid dwn.	Launched.	Completed.
RO.114.	Kawasaki Kobe.	Unknown.	1943.	Unknown.

Fate: Sunk. 17-06-44. By US Forces in the Pacific.

Number.	Builder.	Laid dwn.	Launched.	Completed.
RO.115.	Kawasaki Kobe.	Unknown.	1943.	Unknown.

Fate: Sunk. By US Forces in the Pacific.

Number.	Builder.	Laid dwn.	Launched.	Completed.
RO.116.	Kawasaki Kobe.	Unknown.	1943.	Unknown.

Fate: Sunk. 24-05-44. By US Forces in the Pacific.

Number.	Builder.	Laid dwn.	Launched.	Completed.
RO.117.	Kawasaki Kobe.	Unknown.	1943.	Unknown.

Fate: Sunk. 17-06-44. By US Forces in the Pacific.

SS. (Class).

Displacement. 429/493 Tonnes.		Compliment: 21.	

Dimensions: 146'0" x 20'0" x 13'3".
Machinery: 1 Shaft Diesel/Electric Motors. 400Bhp/150Bhp = 10'0/5.0Kts.
Fuel Cap: Diesel, Unknown.
Armour: None.
Armament: 1 x 25mm AA,

Number.	Builder.	Laid dwn.	Launched.	Completed.
HA.101.	Kawasaki Tanagawa.	Unknown.	1944.	Unknown.

Fate: BU. 1946.

Number.	Builder.	Laid dwn.	Launched.	Completed.
HA.102.	Mitsibushi Kobe.	Unknown.	1944.	Unknown.

Fate: BU. 1946.

Number.	Builder.	Laid dwn.	Launched.	Completed.
HA.103.	Mitsibushi Kobe.	Unknown.	1944.	Unknown.

Fate: Scuttled. 01-04-46.

SUBMARINES. (Continued).

KS. (Class). (Continued).

Number.	Builder.	Laid dwn.	Launched.	Completed.
HA.104.	Kawasaki Tanagawa.	Unknown.	1944.	Unknown.

Fate:: BU. 1946.

Number.	Builder.	Laid dwn.	Launched.	Completed.
HA.105.	Kawasaki Tanagawa.	Unknown.	1945.	Unknown.

Fate: Scuttled. 01-04-46.

Number.	Builder.	Laid dwn.	Launched.	Completed.
HA.106.	Kawasaki Tanagawa.	Unknown.	1944.	Unknown.

Fate: Scuttled. 01-04-46.

Number.	Builder.	Laid dwn.	Launched.	Completed.
HA.107.	Kawasaki Tanagawa.	Unknown.	1945.	Unknown.

Fate: Scuttled. 01-04-46.

Number.	Builder.	Laid dwn.	Launched.	Completed.
HA.108.	Kawasaki Tanagawa.	Unknown.	1945.	Unknown.

Fate: Scuttled. 01-04-46.

Number.	Builder.	Laid dwn.	Launched.	Completed.
HA.109.	Mitsibushi Kobe.	Unknown.	1945.	Unknown.

Fate: Scuttled. 01-04-46.

Number.	Builder.	Laid dwn.	Launched.	Completed.
HA.110.	Kawasaki Tanagawa.	Unknown.	1945.	Unknown.

Fate: Sunk. 16-10-46.

Number.	Builder.	Laid dwn.	Launched.	Completed.
HA.111.	Mitsibushi Kobe.	Unknown.	1945.	Unknown.

Fate: Scuttled. 01-04-46.

Number.	Builder.	Laid dwn.	Launched.	Completed.
HA.112.	Mitsibushi Kobe.	Unknown.	1945.	Unknown.

Fate: BU. 1946.

YU.1. (Class). Small transport S/m's (1943-44).

Displacement. 273/370 Tonnes. Compliment: 13.
Dimensions: 134'2" x 12'10" x 9'8".
Machinery: 1 Shaft Diesel/Electric Motors. 400Bhp/75Shp = 10'0/5.0Kts.
Fuel Cap: Diesel, Unknown.
Armour: None.
Armament: 1 x 37mm AA,

Number.	Builder.	Laid dwn.	Launched.	Completed.
YU.1 -10.	Unknown.	Unknown.	Unknown.	Unknown.

Fate: Sunk. Cause unknown.

SUBMARINES. IContinued).

YU.1. (Class). (Continued).

Number.	Builder.	Laid dwn.	Launched.	Completed.
YU.11-12.	Unknown.	Unknown.	Unknown.	Unknown.

Fate: BU 1947.

YU.1001. (Class). Small transport S/m's (1943-44).

Displacement. 273/370 Tonnes.   **Compliment:** Unknown..
Dimensions: 160'9" x 49'0" x 8'9".
Machinery: 1 Shaft Diesel/Electric Motors. 700Bhp/?Shp = 12'0/?Kts.
Fuel Cap: Diesel, Unknown.
Armour: None.
Armament: Unknown.

Number.	Builder.	Laid dwn.	Launched.	Completed.
YU.1001 -1007.	Unknown.	Unknown.	Unknown.	Unknown.

Fate: Sunk. Cause unknown.

Number.	Builder.	Laid dwn.	Launched.	Completed.
YU1008 - 1014.	Unknown.	Unknown.	Unknown.	Unknown.

Fate: BU 1947 - 48.

S.T.S. (Class).

Displacement. 377/440 Tonnes.   **Compliment:** 22.
Dimensions: 173'11" x 13'1" x 11'3".
Machinery: 1 Shaft Diesel/Electric Motors. 400Bhp/1200Shp = 10'5/13Kts.
Fuel Cap: Diesel, Unknown.
Armour: None.
Armament: 1 x 7.7mm mg. AA. 2 x 21"TT.

Number.	Builder.	Laid dwn.	Launched.	Completed.
HA.201.	Sasebo Navy yd.	Unknown.	1945.	Unknown.

Fate: Scuttled 01-04-46.

Number.	Builder.	Laid dwn.	Launched.	Completed.
HA.202.	Sasebo Navy yd.	Unknown.	1945.	Unknown.

Fate: Scuttled 01-04-46.

Number.	Builder.	Laid dwn.	Launched.	Completed.
HA.203.	Sasebo Navy yd.	Unknown.	1945.	Unknown.

Fate: BU 1948.

Number.	Builder.	Laid dwn.	Launched.	Completed.
HA.204.	sasebo Navy yd.	Unknown.	1945.	Unknown.

Fate. Sunk. 25-10-45. Believed to have foundered during a storm.

Number.	Builder.	Laid dwn.	Launched.	Completed.
HA.205.	Sasebo Navy yd.	Unknown.	1945.	Unknown.

Fate: BU 1946.

SUBMARINES. Continued).

S.T.S. (Class). (Continued).

Number.	Builder.	Laid dwn.	Launched.	Completed.
HA.206.	Kawasaki Tanagawa.	Unknown.	10-07-45.	Unknown.

Fate: Sunk. 25-08-45. Believed to have foundered during a storm.

Number.	Builder.	Laid dwn.	Launched.	Completed.
HA.207.	Sasebo Navy yd.	Unknown.	1945.	Unknown.

Fate: Scuttled. 05-04-46.

Number.	Builder.	Laid dwn.	Launched.	Completed.
HA.208.	Sasebo Navy yd.	Unknown.	1945.	Unknown.

Fate: Scuttled. 01-04-46.

Number.	Builder.	Laid dwn.	Launched.	Completed.
HA.209.	Sasebo Navy yd.	Unknown.	1945.	Unknown.

Fate: BU 1946.

Number.	Builder.	Laid dwn.	Launched.	Completed.
HA.210.	Sasebo Navy yd.	Unknown.	1945.	Unknown.

Fate: Scuttled. 05-04-46.

Number.	Builder.	Laid dwn.	Launched.	Completed.
HA.211.	Kawasaki Tanagawa.	Unknown.	24-04-46.	Unknown.

Fate: BU 1946.

Number.	Builder.	Laid dwn.	Launched.	Completed.
HA.212.	Kawasaki Kobe.	Unknown.	26-06-45.	Unknown.

Fate: BU 1946.

Number.	Builder.	Laid dwn.	Launched.	Completed.
HA.213.	Mitsibushi Kobe.	Unknown.	29-07-45.	Unknown.

Fate: BU 1946.

Number.	Builder.	Laid dwn.	Launched.	Completed.
HA.214.	Mitsibushi Kobe.	Unknown.	15-08-45.	Unknown.

Fate: BU 1946.

Number.	Builder.	Laid dwn.	Launched.	Completed.
HA.215.	Sasebo Navy yd.	Unknown.	15-06-45.	Unknown.

Fate: Scuttled 05-04-46.

Number.	Builder.	Laid dwn.	Launched.	Completed.
HA.216.	Sasebo Navy yd.	Unknown.	1945.	Unknown.

Fate: Scuttled 1946.

Number.	Builder.	Laid dwn.	Launched.	Completed.
HA.217.	Sasebo Navy yd.	Unknown.	26-06-45.	Unknown.

Fate: Scuttled 05-04-46.

SUBMARINES. Continued).

S.T.S. (Class). (Continued).

Number.	Builder.	Laid dwn.	Launched.	Completed.
HA.218.	Sasebo Navy yd.	Unknown.	02-07-45.	Unknown.

Fate: BU 1946

Number.	Builder.	Laid dwn.	Launched.	Completed.
HA.219.	Sasebo Navy yd.	Unknown.	12-07-45.	Unknown.

Fate: Scuttled 05-04-46.

Number.	Builder.	Laid dwn.	Launched.	Completed.
HA.220. NONE.				

Fate:

Number.	Builder.	Laid dwn.	Launched.	Completed.
HA.221.	Kawasaki Kobe.	Unknown.	04-08-45.	Unknown.

Fate: BU 1946.

HA.222.-HA.227, No information available.

Number.	Builder.	Laid dwn.	Launched.	Completed.
HA.228.	Sasebo Navy yd.	Unknown.	18-07-45.	Unknown.

Fate: Scuttled 05-04-46.

Number.	Builder.	Laid dwn.	Launched.	Completed.
HA.229.	Sasebo Navy yd.	Unknown.	27-07-45.	Unknown.

Fate: BU 1946.

Number.	Builder.	Laid dwn.	Launched.	Completed.
HA.230.	Sasebo Navy yd.	Unknown.	1945.	Unknown.

Fate: BU 1946.

SUBMARINES. (Continued).

Ex German & Italian submarines used by the Japanese Navy.

Number.	Builder.	Laid dwn.	Launched.	Completed.
RO.500	(Ex U.511).	Unknown.	Unknown.	Unknown.

Fate: BU 1946.

Number.	Builder.	Laid dwn.	Launched.	Completed.
RO.501.	(Ex U.1224).	Unknown.	Unknown.	Unknown.

Fate: Sunk. 13-05-44. By U.S. Forces off the Azores.

Number.	Builder.	Laid dwn.	Launched.	Completed.
I.501.	(Ex U.181).	Unknown.	Unknown.	Unknown.

Fate: Scuttled or BU 1946-47.

Number.	Builder.	Laid dwn.	Launched.	Completed.
I.502.	(Ex U.862).	Unknown.	Unknown.	Unknown.

Fate: Scuttled or BU 1946-47.

Number.	Builder.	Laid dwn.	Launched.	Completed.
I.505.	(Ex U.219.	Unknown.	Unknown.	Unknown.

Fate: Scuttled or BU 1946-47

Number.	Builder.	Laid dwn.	Launched.	Completed.
I.506.	(Ex U.195).	Unknown.	Unknown.	Unknown.

Fate: Scuttled or BU 1946-47.

Italian boats still in Japanese ports when ITALY surrendered, were handed over to the German navy. In May 45 they were incorporated into the Japanese Navy.

Number.	Builder.	Laid dwn.	Launched.	Completed.
I.503.	(Ex UIT.24).	Unknown.	Unknown.	Unknown.

Fate: Ex Commandante CAPELLINI. Scuttled. 15-04-46.

Number.	Builder.	Laid dwn.	Launched.	Completed.
I.504.	(Ex UIT.25).	Unknown.	Unknown.	Unknown.

Fate: Ex Commandante LUIGI TORELLI. Scuttled. 16-06-46.

PATROL BOATS. (Escort Type).

SHIMUSHU. (Class A).
Displacement. 860/1,004 Tonnes.   Compliment: 150.
Dimensions: 255'0" x 29'10" x 10'0".
Machinery: 2 Shaft Diesel/Electric Motors. 44,200Bhp = 19.7Kts.
Fuel Cap: Diesel, Unknown.
Armour: None.
Armament: 3 x 4.7", 15 x 25mm AA, 60 x DC.
NB: Armament modified to above between 1942-43.

Name.	Builder.	Laid dwn.	Launched.	Completed.
SHIMUSHU.	Mitsu, Tamano.	Unknown.	1939-40.	Unknown.

Fate: To USSR 1947.

Name.	Builder.	Laid dwn.	Launched.	Completed.
HACHIJO.	Sasebo Navy yd.	Unknown.	1939-40.	Unknown.

Fate: BU. 1948.

Name.	Builder.	Laid dwn.	Launched.	Completed.
KUNASHIRI.	Tsurumi Yokohama.	Unknown.	1939-40.	Unknown.

Fate: Sunk. 04-06-46. Wrecked. Cause unknown.

Name.	Builder.	Laid dwn.	Launched.	Completed.
ISHIKAKI.	Mitsu, Tamano.	Unknown.	1939-40.	Unknown.

Fate: Sunk. 31-05-44. Cause unknown.

ETOROFU (Class. Improved Type).
Displacement. 870/1,004 Tonnes.   Compliment: 147.
Dimensions: 255'0" x 29'10" x 10'0".
Machinery: 2 Shaft Diesel/Electric Motors. 44,200Bhp = 19.7Kts.
Fuel Cap: Diesel, Unknown.
Armour: None.
Armament: 3 x 4.7", 15 x 25mm AA, 60 x DC, 1 x 3" DC Thrower.
NB: Armament modified to above between 1942 - 43.
KANJU. Only 2 x 4.7" Main-armament.

Name.	Builder.	Laid dwn.	Launched.	Completed.
ETOROFU.	Hitachi Sakurajima.	Unknown.	1942-43.	Unknown.

Fate: To USA. BU 1947.

Name.	Builder.	Laid dwn.	Launched.	Completed.
OKI.	Uraga Tokyo.	Unknown.	1942-43.	Unknown.

Fate: To China. 1947 renamed KU AN.

Name.	Builder.	Laid dwn.	Launched.	Completed.
SADO.	Tsurumi Tamano.	Unknown.	1942-43.	Unknown.

Fate: Sunk. 22-08-44. Cause unknown.

Name.	Builder.	Laid dwn.	Launched.	Completed.
MATSUWA.	Mitsui Tamano.	Unknown.	1942-43.	Unknown.

Fate: Sunk. 22-08-44. Torpedoed by US S/m.

PATROL BOATS. (Continued).

ETOROFU (Class. Improved Type). (Continued).

Name.	Builder.	Laid dwn.	Launched.	Completed.
MUTSURE.	Hitachi Sakurajima.	Unknown.	1942-43.	Unknown.

Fate: Sunk. 02-09-43. Torpedoed by US S/m.

Name.	Builder.	Laid dwn.	Launched.	Completed.
WAKAMIJA.	Mitsui Tamano.	Unknown.	1942-43.	Unknown

Fate: Sunk. 23-11-43. Torpedoed by US S/m.

Name.	Builder.	Laid dwn.	Launched.	Completed.
HIRADO.	Hitachi Sakurajima.	Unknown.	1942-43.	Unknown.

Fate: Sunk. 12-09-44. Torpedoed by US S/m.

Name.	Builder.	Laid dwn.	Launched.	Completed.
IKI.	Mitsui Tamano.	Unknown.	1942-43.	Unknown

Fate: Sunk. 24-05-44. Torpedoed by US S/m.

Name.	Builder.	Laid dwn.	Launched.	Completed.
KASADO.	Urago Tokyo.	Unknown.	1942-43.	Unknown.

Fate: BU. 1948.

Name.	Builder.	Laid dwn.	Launched.	Completed.
KANJU.	Urago Tokyo.	Unknown.	1942-43.	Unknown.

Fate: Sunk. 15-08-45. By USSR Forces.

Name.	Builder.	Laid dwn.	Launched.	Completed.
AMAKUSA.	Hitachi Sakurajima.	Unknown.	1942-43.	Unknown.

Fate: Sunk. 09-08-45. By US A/c.

PATROL BOATS & ESCORTS.

MIKURA. (Class Type B).

Displacement. 1,004 Tonnes.	Compliment: 147.

Dimensions: 258'5" x 29'10'' x 9'10".
Machinery: 2 Shaft Diesel/Electric Motors. 44,200Bhp = 19.5Kts.
Fuel Cap: Diesel, Unknown.
Armour: None.
Armament: 3 x 4.7", 4 x 25mm AA, 120 x DC.

Name.	Builder.	Laid dwn.	Launched.	Completed.
MIKURA.	Tsurumi Yokohama.	Unknown.	1943-44.	Unknown.

Fate: Lost. 02-05-45? Cause unknown.

Name.	Builder.	Laid dwn.	Launched.	Completed.
AWAJI.	Hitachi Sakurajima.	Unknown.	1943-44.	Unknown.

Fate: Sunk. 02-06-44. Torpedoed by US S/m.

Name.	Builder.	Laid dwn.	Launched.	Completed.
NOMI.	Tsurumi Yokohama.	Unknown.	1943-44.	Unknown.

Fate: Sunk. 15-04-45. Torpedoed by US S/m.

PATROL BOATS & ESCORTS.

MIKURA. (Class Type B Escorts.

Name.	Builder.	Laid dwn.	Launched.	Completed.
NOMI.	Tsurumi Yokohama.	Unknown.	1943-44.	Unknown.

Fate. Sunk. 12-01-43. Torpedoed by US S/m.

Name.	Builder.	Laid dwn.	Launched.	Completed.
KUSAGAKI.	Tsurami Yokohama.	Unknown.	1943-44.	Unknown.

Fate: Sunk. 07-08-44. Torpedoed by US S/m.

Name.	Builder.	Laid dwn.	Launched.	Completed.
KURAHASHI.	Tsurami Yokohama.	Unknown.	1943-44.	Unknown.

Fate: To UK. 1947. BU.

Name.	Builder.	Laid dwn.	Launched.	Completed.
YASHIRO.	Hitachi Sakurajima.	Unknown.	1943-44.	Unknown.

Fate: To CHINA. 1947. Renamed CHENG AN.

UKURU. (Class. Improved Type B).

Displacement. 1,004 Tonnes.   Compliment: 147.
Dimensions: 258'5" x 29'10" x 9'10".
Machinery: 2 Shaft Diesel/Electric Motors. 44,200Bhp = 19.5Kts.
Fuel Cap: Diesel, Unknown.
Armour: None.
Armament: 3 x 4.7", 6 x 25mm AA, 120 x DC.

Name.	Builder.	Laid dwn.	Launched.	Completed.
UKURU.	Tsurumi Yokohama.	Unknown.	1944-45.	Unknown.

Fate: To JMSDF. 1948.

Name.	Builder.	Laid dwn.	Launched.	Completed.
HIBURI.	Hitachi Sakurajima.	Unknown.	1944-45.	Unknown.

Fate: Sunk. 22-08-44. Torpedoed by US S/m.

Name.	Builder.	Laid dwn.	Launched.	Completed.
SHONAN.	Hitachi Sakurajima.	Unknown.	1944-45.	Unknown.

Fate: Sunk. 25-02-45. Torpedoed by US S/m.

Name.	Builder.	Laid dwn.	Launched.	Completed.
DAITO.	Hitachi Sakurajima.	Unknown.	1944-45.	Unknown.

Fate: Lost. 16-11-45. Mined post war.

Name.	Builder.	Laid dwn.	Launched.	Completed.
OKINAWA.	Tsurumi Yokohama.	Unknown.	1944-45.	

Fate: Sunk. 30-07-45. By US A/c.

Name.	Builder.	Laid dwn.	Launched.	Completed.
KUME.	Hitachi Sakurajima.	Unknown.	1944-45.	Unknown.

Fate: Sunk. 28-01-45. Torpedoed by US S/m.

PATROL BOATS & ESCORTS.

UKURA. (Class Improved Type B). (Continued).

Name.	Builder.	Laid dwn.	Launched.	Completed.
IKUNA.	Hitachi Sakurajima.	Unknown.	1944-45.	Unknown.

Fate: To JMSDF. 1948.

Name.	Builder.	Laid dwn.	Launched.	Completed.
SHINAN.	Uraga Tokyo.	Unknown.	1944-45.	Unknown.

Fate: To JMSDF. 1948.

Name.	Builder.	Laid dwn.	Launched.	Completed.
YAKU.	Uraga Tokyo.	Unknown.	1944-45.	Unknown.

Fate: Sunk. 23-02-45. Torpedoed by US S/m.

Name.	Builder.	Laid dwn.	Launched.	Completed.
AGUNI.	Tsurumi Yokohama.	Unknown.	1944-45.	Unknown.

Fate: BU. 1948.

Name.	Builder.	Laid dwn.	Launched.	Completed.
MOKUTO.	Hitachi Sakurajima.	Unknown.	1944-45.	Unknown.

Fate: Sunk. 04-04-45. Torpedoed by US S/m.

Name.	Builder.	Laid dwn.	Launched.	Completed.
INAGI.	Mitsui Tamano.	Unknown.	1944-45.	Unknown.

Fate: Sunk. 09-08-45. By US A/c.

Name.	Builder.	Laid dwn.	Launched.	Completed.
UKU.	Sasebo Navy yd.	Unknown.	1944-45.	Unknown.

Fate: To USA. 1947. BU.

Name.	Builder.	Laid dwn.	Launched.	Completed.
CHIKUBU.	Urago Tokyo.	Unknown.	1944-45.	Unknown.

Fate: To JMSDF. 1948.

Name.	Builder.	Laid dwn.	Launched.	Completed.
HABUSHI.	Mitsui Tamano.	Unknown.	1944-45.	Unknown.

Fate: To USA. 1947. BU.

Name.	Builder.	Laid dwn.	Launched.	Completed.
SAKITO.	Hitachi Sakurajima.	Unknown.	1944-45.	Unknown.

Fate: To USA. 1947. BU.

Name.	Builder.	Laid dwn.	Launched.	Completed.
KUGA.	Sasebo Navy yd.	Unknown.	1944-45.	Unknown.

Fate: BU. 1948.

Name.	Builder.	Laid dwn.	Launched.	Completed.
OGA.	Mitsui Tamano.	Unknown.	1944-45.	Unknown.

Fate: Sunk. 02-04-45. Cause unknown.

PATROL BOATS & ESCORTS. (Continued).

UKURU. (Class. Improved Type B). (Continued).

Name.	Builder.	Laid dwn.	Launched.	Completed.
KOZU.	Uraga Tokyo.	Unknown.	1944-45.	Unknown.

Fate: To USSR. 1947.

Name.	Builder.	Laid dwn.	Launched.	Completed.
KANAWA.	Mitsui Tamano.	Unknown.	1944-45.	Unknown.

Fate: To UK. 1947. BU.

Name.	Builder.	Laid dwn.	Launched.	Completed.
SHIGA.	Sasebo Navy yd.	Unknown.	1944-45.	Unknown.

Fate: To JMSDF. 1948.

Name.	Builder.	Laid dwn.	Launched.	Completed.
ANAMI.	Tsurumi Yokohama.	Unknown.	1944-45.	Unknown.

Fate: To UK. 1947. BU.

Name.	Builder.	Laid dwn.	Launched.	Completed.
HODAKA.	Uraga Tokyo.	Unknown.	1944-45.	Unknown.

Fate: To USA. 1947. BU 1948.

Name.	Builder.	Laid dwn.	Launched.	Completed.
HABUTO.	Hitachi Sakurajima.	Unknown.	1944-45.	Unknown.

Fate: To UK. 1947. BU.

Name.	Builder.	Laid dwn.	Launched.	Completed.
IWO.	Maizuru Navy yd.	Unknown.	1944-45.	Unknown.

Fate: BU. 1946.

Name.	Builder.	Laid dwn.	Launched.	Completed.
TAKANE.	Mitsui Tamano.	Unknown.	1944-45.	Unknown.

Fate: BU. 1946.

Name.	Builder.	Laid dwn.	Launched.	Completed.
IKARA.	Uraga Tokyo.	Unknown.	1944-45.	Unknown.

Fate: BU. 1946.

Name.	Builder.	Laid dwn.	Launched	Completed.
SHISKA.	Hitachi Sakurajima.	Unknown.	1944-45.	Unknown.

Fate: To CHINA. 1947. Renamed HUI AN.

Name.	Builder.	Laid dwn.	Launched.	Completed.
IKINO.	Uraga Tokyo.	Unknown.	1944-45.	Unknown.

Fate: To USSR. 1947.

Name.	Builder.	Laid dwn.	Launched.	Completed.
OTSU.	Hitachi Sakurajima.	Unknown.	1944-45.	Unknown.

Fate: BU. 1948.

PATROL BOATS & ESCORTS. (Continued).

UKURU. (Class. Improved Type B). (Continued).

Name.	Builder.	Laid dwn.	Launched.	Completed.
URIMA.	Uraga Tokyo.	Unknown.	1944-45.	Unknown.

Fate: BU. 1946.

Name.	Builder.	Laid dwn.	Launched.	Completed.
MUROTSO.	Uraga Tokyo.	Unknown.	1944-45.	Unknown.

Fate: BU. 1946.

Name.	Builder.	Laid dwn.	Launched.	Completed.
TOMISHIRA.	Sakurajima Osaka.	Unknown.	Unfinished.	Unknown.

Fate: BU. Unlaunched. 1947.

UKURU. (Class. Type C).

Displacement. 797 Tonnes.   Compliment: 136.
Dimensions: 221'5" x 27'7" x 9'4".
Machinery: 2 Shaft Diesels. 1,900Bhp = 16.5Kts.
Fuel Cap: Diesel, Unknown.
Armour: None.
Armament: 2 x 4.7", 16 x 25mm AA, 120 x DC.
NB:- Builders of particular units are not generally known. Yards are as follows-
Miysibushi Kobe, Kyowa Osaka, Nihonkai Toyama, Tsurumi Yokohama,
Maizuru Navy yd, Naniwaosaka Niigata.

Number.	Builder.	Laid dwn.	Launched.	Completed.
001.	See above list.	Unknown.	Unknown.	Unknown.

Fate: Sunk. 09-01-45. Cause unknown.

Number.	Builder.	Laid dwn.	Launched.	Completed.
003.	See above list.	Unknown.	Unknown.	Unknown.

Fate: Sunk. 09-01-45. Cause unknown.

Number.	Builder.	Laid dwn.	Launched.	Completed.
005.	See above list.	Unknown.	Unknown.	Unknown.

Fate: Sunk. 21-09-45. Cause unknown.

Number.	Builder.	Laid dwn.	Launched.	Completed.
007.	See above list.	Unknown.	Unknown.	Unknown.

Fate: Sunk. 10-11-44. Cause unknown.

Number.	Builder.	Laid dwn.	Launched.	Completed.
009.	See above list.	Unknown.	Unknown.	Unknown.

Fate: Sunk. 14-02-45. Cause unknown.

Number.	Builder.	Laid dwn.	Launched.	Completed.
011.	See above list.	Unknown.	Unknown.	Unknown.

Fate: Sunk. 10-11-44. Cause unknown.

ESCORTS & PATROL BOATS (Continued).

UKURU. (Class. Type C). (Continued).

Number.	Builder.	Laid dwn.	Launched.	Completed.
013.	See above list.	Unknown.	Unknown.	Unknown.

Fate: Sunk. 14-08-44. Cause unknown.

Number.	Builder.	Laid dwn.	Launched	Completed.
015.	See above list.	Unknown.	Unknown.	Unknown.

Fate: Sunk. 06-06-44. Cause unknown.

Number.	Builder.	Laid dwn.	Launched.	Completed.
017.	See above list.	Unknown.	Unknown.	Unknown.

Fate: Sunk. 12-01-45. Cause unknown.

Number.	Builder.	Laid dwn.	Launched.	Completed.
019.	See above list.	Unknown.	Unknown.	Unknown.

Fate: Sunk. 12-01-45. Cause unknown.

Number.	Builder.	Laid dwn.	Launched.	Completed.
021.	See above list.	Unknown.	Unknown.	Unknown.

Fate: Sunk. 06-10-45. Cause unknown.

Number.	Builder.	Laid dwn.	Launched.	Completed.
023.	See above list.	Unknown.	Unknown.	Unknown.

Fate: Sunk. 12-01-45. Cause unknown.

Number.	Builder.	Laid dwn.	Launched.	Completed.
025.	See above list.	Unknown.	Unknown.	Unknown.

Fate: Probably sunk. 03-05-45. Cause unknown.

Number.	Builder.	Laid dwn.	Launched.	Completed.
027.	See above list.	Unknown.	Unknown.	Unknown.

Fate: To UK. BU. 1947.

Number.	Builder.	Laid dwn.	Launched.	Completed.
029.	See above list.	Unknown.	Unknown.	Unknown.

Fate: BU. 1948.

Number.	Builder.	Laid dwn.	Launched.	Completed.
031.	See above list.	Unknown.	Unknown.	Unknown.

Fate: Sunk. 14-04-45. Cause unknown.

Number.	Builder.	Laid dwn.	Launched.	Completed.
033.	See above list.	Unknown.	Unknown.	Unknown.

Fate: Sunk. 28-03-45. Cause unknown.

Number.	Builder.	Laid dwn.	Launched.	Completed.
035.	See above list.	Unknown.	Unknown.	Unknown.

Fate: Sunk. 12-01-45. Cause unknown.

PATROL BOATS & ESCORTS. (Continued).

UKURU. (Class. Type C). (Continued).

Number.	Builder.	Laid dwn.	Launched.	Completed.
037.	See above list.	Unknown.	Unknown.	Unknown.

Fate: To USA. 1947. BU.

Number.	Builder.	Laid dwn.	Launched.	Completed.
039.	See above list.	Unknown.	Unknown.	Unknown.

Fate: Sunk. 07-08-45. Cause unknown.

Number.	Builder.	Laid dwn.	Launched.	Completed.
041.	See above list.	Unknown.	Unknown.	Unknown.

Fate: Sunk. 09-06-45. Cause unknown.
Page 69.

Number.	Builder.	Laid dwn.	Launched.	Completed.
043.	See above list.	Unknown.	Unknown.	Unknown.

Fate: Sunk. 12-01-45. Cause unknown.

Number.	Builder.	Laid dwn.	Launched.	Completed.
045.	See above list.	Unknown.	Unknown.	Unknown.

Fate: BU. 1948.

Number.	Builder.	Laid dwn.	Launched.	Completed.
047.	See above list.	Unknown.	Unknown.	Unknown.

Fate: Sunk. 14-08-45. Cause unknown.

Number.	Builder.	Laid dwn.	Launched.	Completed.
049.	See above list.	Unknown.	Unknown.	Unknown.

Fate: To USA. 1947. BU.

Number.	Builder.	Laid dwn.	Launched.	Completed.
051.	See above list.	Unknown.	Unknown.	Unknown.

Fate: Sunk. 12-01-45. Cause unknown.

Number.	Builder.	Laid dwn.	Launched.	Completed.
053.	See above list.	Unknown.	Unknown.	Unknown.

Fate: Sunk. 07-02-45. Cause unknown.

Number.	Builder.	Laid dwn.	Launched.	Completed.
055.	See above list.	Unknown.	Unknown.	Unknown.

Fate: To UK. BU. 1947.

Number.	Builder.	Laid dwn.	Launched.	Completed.
057.	See above list.	Unknown.	Unknown.	Unknown.

Fate: BU. 1947.

Number.	Builder.	Laid dwn.	Launched.	Completed.
059.	See above list.	Unknown.	Unknown.	Unknown.

Fate: BU. 1947.

PATROL BOATS & ESCORTS. (Continued).

UKURU. (Class. Type C). (Continued).

Number.	Builder.	Laid dwn.	Launched.	Completed.
061.	See above list.	Unknown.	Unknown.	Unknown,

Fate: BU. 1946.

Number.	Builder.	Laid dwn.	Launched.	Completed.
063.	See above list.	Unknown.	Unknown.	Unknown.

Fate: BU. 1948.

Number.	Builder.	Laid dwn.	Launched.	Completed.
065.	See above list.	Unknown.	Unknown.	Unknown.

Fate: Sunk. 14-07-45. Cause unknown.

Number.	Builder.	Laid dwn.	Launched.	Completed.
067.	See above list.	Unknown.	Unknown.	Unknown.

Fate: To CHINA. 1947. Renamed YING KU..

Number.	Builder.	Laid dwn.	Launched.	Completed.
069.	See above list.	Unknown.	Unknown.	Unknown.

Fate: Sunk. 16-03-45. Cause unknown.

Number.	Builder.	Laid dwn.	Launched.	Completed.
071.	See above list.	Unknown.	Unknown.	Unknown.

Fate: To USSR. 1947.

Number.	Builder.	Laid dwn.	Launched.	Completed.
073.	See above list.	Unknown.	Unknown.	Unknown.

Fate: Sunk. 16-04-45. Cause unknown.

Number.	Builder.	Laid dwn.	Launched.	Completed.
075.	See above list.	Unknown.	Unknown.	Unknown.

Fate: Lost after. 23-08-45. Cause unknown.

Number.	Builder.	Laid dwn.	Launched.	Completed.
077.	See above list.	Unknown.	Unknown.	Unknown.

Fate: To USSR. 1947.

Number.	Builder.	Laid dwn.	Launched.	Completed.
079.	See above list.	Unknown.	Unknown.	Unknown.

Fate: To USSR. 1947.

Number.	Builder.	Laid dwn.	Launched.	Completed.
081.	See above list.	Unknown.	Unknown.	Unknown.

Fate: To CHINA. 1947. Renamed MUKDEN.

Number.	Builder.	Laid dwn.	Launched.	Completed.
083.	See above list.	Unknown.	Unknown.	Unknown.

Fate: BU. 1948.

UKURU. (Class. Type C). (Continued).

Number.	Builder.	Laid dwn.	Launched.	Completed.
085.	See above list.	Unknown.	Unknown.	Unknown.

Fate: To CHINA. 1947. Renamed SHIN AN.

Number.	Builder.	Laid dwn.	Launched.	Completed.
087.	See above list.	Unknown.	Unknown.	Unknown.

Fate: To USA. 1947. BU.

Number.	Builder.	Laid dwn.	Launched.	Completed.
089.	See above list.	Unknown.	Unknown.	Unknown.

Fate: BU incomplete. 1948.

Number.	Builder.	Laid dwn.	Launched.	Completed.
095.	See above list.	Unknown.	Unknown.	Unknown.

Fate: BU. 1948.

Number.	Builder.	Laid dwn.	Launched.	Completed.
097.	See above list.	Unknown.	Unknown.	Unknown.

Fate: BU incomplete. 1947.

Number.	Builder.	Laid dwn.	Launched.	Completed.
105.	See above list.	Unknown.	Unknown.	Unknown.

Fate: To USSR. 1947.

Number.	Builder.	Laid dwn.	Launched.	Completed.
107.	See above list.	Unknown.	Unknown.	Unknown.

Fate: To CHINA. 1947. Renamed CHAO AN.

Number.	Builder.	Laid dwn.	Launched.	Completed.
205.	See above list.	Unknown.	Unknown.	Unknown.

Fate: To CHINA. 1947. Renamed CHANG AN.

Number.	Builder.	Laid dwn.	Launched.	Completed.
207.	See above list.	Unknown.	Unknown.	Unknown.

Fate: To USA. 1947. BU.

Number.	Builder.	Laid dwn.	Launched.	Completed.
213.	See above list.	Unknown.	Unknown.	Unknown.

Fate: Sunk. 18-08-45. Cause unknown.

Number.	Builder.	Laid dwn.	Launched.	Completed.
215.	See above list.	Unknown.	Unknown.	Unknown.

Fate: To CHINA. 1947. Renamed LIAO HAI.

Number.	Builder.	Laid dwn.	Launched.	Completed.
217.	See above list.	Unknown.	Unknown.	Unknown.

Fate: To UK. 1947. BU.

UKURU. (Class. Type C). (Continued).

Number.	Builder.	Laid dwn.	Launched.	Completed.
219.	See above list.	Unknown.	Unknown.	Unknown,

Fate: Sunk. 15-07-45. Cause unknown.

Number.	Builder.	Laid dwn.	Launched.	Completed.
221.	See above list.	Unknown.	Unknown.	Unknown.

Fate: To USSR. 1947.

Number.	Builder.	Laid dwn.	Launched.	Completed.
223.	See above list.	Unknown.	Unknown.	Unknown.

Fate: BU incomplete. 1947.

Number.	Builder.	Laid dwn.	Launched.	Completed.
225.	See above list.	Unknown.	Unknown.	Unknown.

Fate: BU. 1948.

Number.	Builder.	Laid dwn.	Launched.	Completed.
227.	See above list.	Unknown.	Unknown.	Unknown.

Fate: To USSR. 1947.

Number.	Builder.	Laid dwn.	Launched.	Completed.
093.	See above list.	Unknown.	Unknown.	Unknown.

Fate: Demolished on slipway. 1945.

Number.	Builder.	Laid dwn.	Launched.	Completed.
101.	See above list.	Unknown.	Unknown.	Unknown.

Fate: Demolished on slipway. 1945.

Number.	Builder.	Laid dwn.	Launched.	Completed.
109.	See above list.	Unknown.	Unknown.	Unknown.

Fate: Demolished on slipway. 1945.

Number.	Builder.	Laid dwn.	Launched.	Completed.
117.	See above list.	Unknown.	Unknown.	Unknown.

Fate: Demolished on slipway. 1945.

Number.	Builder.	Laid dwn.	Launched.	Completed.
229.	See above list.	Unknown.	Unknown.	Unknown.

Fate: Demolished on slipway. 1945.

Number.	Builder.	Laid dwn.	Launched.	Completed.
235.	See above list.	Unknown.	Unknown.	Unknown.

Fate: Demolished on slipway. 1945.

PATROL BOATS & ESCORTS. (Continued).

UKURU. (Class. Type D).
Displacement. 9,240 Tonnes.   **Compliment: Unknown.**
Dimensions: 228'0" x 28'2" x 10'0".
Machinery: 1 Shaft geared Turbine, 2 Boilers, 2,500Bhp = 17.5Kts.
Fuel Cap: Unknown.
Armour: None.
Armament: 2 x 4.7", 16 x 25mm AA, 120 x DC, 1 3" DCT.
NB:- Builders of particular units are not generally known. Yards are as follows-
Mitsibushi Nagasaki, Kawasaki Kobe, Ishikawajima Tokyo.

Number.	Builder.	Laid dwn.	Launched.	Completed.
002.	See above list.	Unknown.	Unknown.	Unknown.

Fate: BU. 1948.

Number.	Builder.	Laid dwn.	Launched.	Completed.
004.	See above list.	Unknown.	Unknown.	Unknown.

Fate: BU. 1948.

Number.	Builder.	Laid dwn.	Launched.	Completed.
006.	See above list.	Unknown.	Unknown.	Unknown.

Fate. Sunk. 13-08-45. Cause unknown.

Number.	Builder.	Laid dwn.	Launched.	Completed.
008.	See above list.	Unknown.	Unknown.	Unknown.

Fate: To UK. 1947. BU.

Number.	Builder.	Laid dwn.	Launched.	Completed.
010.	See above list.	Unknown.	Unknown.	Unknown.

Fate: Sunk. 27-09-44. Cause unknown.

Number.	Builder.	Laid dwn.	Launched.	Completed.
012.	See above list.	Unknown.	Unknown.	Unknown.

Fate: To USA. 1947. BU.

Number.	Builder.	Laid dwn.	Launched.	Completed.
014.	See above list.	Unknown.	Unknown.	Unknown.

Fate. To CHINA. 1947. Renamed CHI NAN.

Number.	Builder.	Laid dwn.	Launched.	Completed.
016.	See above list.	Unknown.	Unknown.	Unknown.

Fate: To UK. 1947. BU.

Number.	Builder.	Laid dwn.	Launched.	Completed.
018.	See above list.	Unknown.	Unknown.	Unknown.

Fate: Sunk. 29-03-45. Cause unknown.

Number.	Builder.	Laid dwn.	Launched.	Completed.
020.	See above list.	Unknown.	Unknown.	Unknown.

Fate: Sunk. 29-12-44. Cause unknown.

PATROL BOATS & ESCORTS. (Continued).

UKURU. (Class. Type D). (Continued).

Number.	Builder.	Laid dwn.	Launched.	Completed.
022.	See above list.	Unknown.	Unknown.	Unknown.

Fate. To USA. 1947. BU.

Number.	Builder.	Laid dwn.	Launched.	Completed.
024.	See above list.	Unknown.	Unknown.	Unknown.

Fate: Sunk. 28-06-44.

Number.	Builder.	Laid dwn.	Launched.	Completed.
026.	See above list.	Unknown.	Unknown.	Unknown.

Fate: To USA. 1947. BU.

Number.	Builder.	Laid dwn.	Launched.	Completed.
028.	See above list.	Unknown.	Unknown.	Unknown.

Fate. Sunk. 14-12-44. Cause unknown.

Number.	Builder.	Laid dwn.	Launched.	Completed.
030.	See above list.	Unknown.	Unknown.	Unknown.

Fate: Sunk. 28-07-45. Cause unknown.

Number.	Builder.	Laid dwn.	Launched.	Completed.
032.	See above list.	Unknown.	Unknown.	Unknown.

Fate: To UK. 1947. BU.

Number.	Builder.	Laid dwn.	Launched.	Completed.
034.	See above list.	Unknown.	Unknown.	Unknown.

Fate: To USSR. 1947.

Number.	Builder.	Laid dwn.	Launched.	Completed.
036.	See above list.	Unknown.	Unknown.	Unknown.

Fate: To USA. 1947. BU.

Number.	Builder.	Laid dwn.	Launched.	Completed.
038.	See above list.	Unknown.	Unknown.	Unknown.

Fate. Sunk. 25-11-44. Cause unknown.

Number.	Builder.	Laid dwn.	Launched.	Completed.
040.	See above list.	Unknown.	Unknown.	Unknown.

Fate: To CHINA. Renamed CHENG AN.

Number.	Builder.	Laid dwn.	Launched.	Completed.
042.	See above list.	Unknown.	Unknown.	Unknown.

Fate: Sunk. 10-01-45.

Number.	Builder.	Laid dwn.	Launched.	Completed.
044.	See above list.	Unknown.	Unknown.	Unknown.

Fate: To USA. 1947. BU.

PATROL BOATS & ESCORTS. (Continued).

UKURU. (Class. Type D). (Continued).

Number.	Builder.	Laid dwn.	Launched.	Completed.
046.	See above list.	Unknown.	Unknown.	Unknown.

Fate: Sunk. 17-08-45. Cause unknown.

Number.	Builder.	Laid dwn.	Launched.	Completed.
048.	See above list.	Unknown.	Unknown.	Unknown.

Fate: To USSR. 1947.

Number.	Builder.	Laid dwn.	Launched.	Completed.
050.	See above list.	Unknown.	Unknown.	Unknown.

Fate: BU. 1948.

Number.	Builder.	Laid dwn.	Launched.	Completed.
052.	See above list.	Unknown.	Unknown.	Unknown.

Fate: To USSR. 1947.

Number.	Builder.	Laid dwn.	Launched.	Completed.
054.	See above list.	Unknown.	Unknown.	Unknown.

Fate: Sunk. 15-12-44. Cause unknown.

Number.	Builder.	Laid dwn.	Launched.	Completed.
056.	See above list.	Unknown.	Unknown.	Unknown.

Fate: Sunk. 17-02-45. Cause unknown.

Number.	Builder.	Laid dwn.	Launched.	Completed.
058.	See above list.	Unknown.	Unknown.	Unknown.

Fate: To USA. 1947. BU.

Number.	Builder.	Laid dwn.	Launched.	Completed.
060.	See above list.	Unknown.	Unknown.	Unknown.

Fate: To UK. 1947. BU.

Number.	Builder.	Laid dwn.	Launched.	Completed.
062.	See above list.	Unknown.	Unknown.	Unknown.

Fate: BU. 1948.

Number.	Builder.	Laid dwn.	Launched.	Completed.
064.	See above list.	Unknown.	Unknown.	Unknown.

Fate: Sunk. 03-12-44. Cause unknown.

Number.	Builder.	Laid dwn.	Launched.	Completed.
072.	See above list.	Unknown.	Unknown.	Unknown.

Fate: Sunk. 01-07-45. Cause unknown.

Number.	Builder.	Laid dwn.	Launched.	Completed.
074.	See above list.	Unknown.	Unknown.	Unknown.

Fate: Sunk. 14-07-45. Cause unknown.

PATROL BOATS & ESCORTS. (Continued).

UKURU. (Class. Type D. (Continued).

Number.	Builder.	Laid dwn.	Launched.	Completed.
076.	See above list.	Unknown.	Unknown.	Unknown,

Fate: To USSR. 1947.

Number.	Builder.	Laid dwn.	Launched.	Completed.
078.	See above list.	Unknown.	Unknown.	Unknown.

Fate: To USSR. 1947.

Number.	Builder.	Laid dwn.	Launched.	Completed.
082..	See above list.	Unknown.	Unknown.	Unknown.

Fate: Sunk. 10-08-45. Cause unknown.

Number.	Builder.	Laid dwn.	Launched.	Completed.
084.	See above list.	Unknown.	Unknown.	Unknown.

Fate: Sunk. 29-03-45. Cause unknown.

Number.	Builder.	Laid dwn.	Launched.	Completed.
102.	See above list.	Unknown.	Unknown.	Unknown.

Fate. To USSR. 1947.

Number.	Builder.	Laid dwn.	Launched.	Completed.
104.	See above list.	Unknown.	Unknown.	Unknown.

Fate: To CHINA. 1947. Renamed TAI AN.

Number.	Builder.	Laid dwn.	Launched.	Completed.
106.	See above list.	Unknown.	Unknown.	Unknown.

Fate. To USA. 1947. BU.

Number.	Builder.	Laid dwn.	Launched.	Completed.
112.	See above list.	Unknown.	Unknown.	Unknown.

Fate. Sunk. 18-07-45. Cause unknown.

Number.	Builder.	Laid dwn.	Launched.	Completed.
116.	See above list.	Unknown.	Unknown.	Unknown.

Fate: BU. 1946.

Number.	Builder.	Laid dwn.	Launched.	Completed.
118.	See above list.	Unknown.	Unknown.	Unknown.

Fate. To CHINA. 1947. Renamed CHIEH 12.

Number.	Builder.	Laid dwn.	Launched.	Completed.
124.	See above list.	Unknown.	Unknown.	Unknown.

Fate. BU. 1948.

Number.	Builder.	Laid dwn.	Launched.	Completed.
126.	See above list.	Unknown.	Unknown.	Unknown.

Fate: To UK. 1947. BU.

PATROL BOATS & ESCORTS. (Continued).

UKURU. (Class. Type D. (Continued).

Number.	Builder.	Laid dwn.	Launched.	Completed.
130.	See above list.	Unknown.	Unknown.	Unknown.

Fate. Sunk. 29-03-45. Cause unknown.

Number.	Builder.	Laid dwn.	Launched.	Completed.
132.	See above list.	Unknown.	Unknown.	Unknown.

Fate. BU. 1948.

Number.	Builder.	Laid dwn.	Launched.	Completed.
134.	See above list.	Unknown.	Unknown.	Unknown.

Fate: Sunk. 06-04-45. Cause unknown.

Number.	Builder.	Laid dwn.	Launched.	Completed.
138.	See above list.	Unknown.	Unknown.	Unknown.

Fate. Sunk. 02-01-45. Cause unknown.

Number.	Builder.	Laid dwn.	Launched.	Completed.
142.	See above list.	Unknown.	Unknown.	Unknown.

Fate: To USSR. 1947.

Number.	Builder.	Laid dwn.	Launched.	Completed.
144.	See above list.	Unknown.	Unknown.	Unknown.

Fate. Sunk. 02-02-45. Cause unknown.

Number.	Builder.	Laid dwn.	Launched.	Completed.
150.	See above list.	Unknown.	Unknown.	Unknown.

Fate: To USA. 1947.

Number.	Builder.	Laid dwn.	Launched.	Completed.
154.	See above list.	Unknown.	Unknown.	Unknown.

Fate. To UK. 1947. BU.

Number.	Builder.	Laid dwn.	Launched.	Completed.
156.	See above list.	Unknown.	Unknown.	Unknown.

Fate: To UK. 1947. BU.

Number.	Builder.	Laid dwn.	Launched.	Completed.
158.	See above list.	Unknown.	Unknown.	Unknown.

Fate. To USA. 1947. BU.

Number.	Builder.	Laid dwn.	Launched.	Completed.
160.	See above list.	Unknown.	Unknown.	Unknown.

Fate: To UK. 1947. BU.

Number.	Builder.	Laid dwn.	Launched.	Completed.
186.	See above list.	Unknown.	Unknown.	Unknown.

Fate. Sunk. 02-04-45. Cause unknown.

UKURU. (Class.Type D). (Continued).

Number.	Builder.	Laid dwn.	Launched.	Completed.
190.	See above list.	Unknown.	Unknown.	Unknown.

Fate: BU. 1948.

Number.	Builder.	Laid dwn.	Launched.	Completed.
192.	See above list.	Unknown.	Unknown.	Unknown.

Fate. To CHINA. 1947. Renamed TUNG AN.

Number.	Builder.	Laid dwn.	Launched.	Completed.
194.	See above list.	Unknown.	Unknown.	Unknown.

Fate: To CHINA. 1947. Renamed CHIEH 6.

Number.	Builder.	Laid dwn.	Launched.	Completed.
196.	See above list.	Unknown.	Unknown.	Unknown.

Fate. To USSR. 1947.

Number.	Builder.	Laid dwn.	Launched.	Completed.
198.	See above list.	Unknown.	Unknown.	Unknown.

Fate. To CHINA. 1947. Renamed CHIEH 14.

Number.	Builder.	Laid dwn.	Launched.	Completed.
200.	See above list.	Unknown.	Unknown.	Unknown.

Fate: BU. 1948.

Number.	Builder.	Laid dwn.	Launched.	Completed.
202.	See above list.	Unknown.	Unknown.	Unknown.

Fate. BU. 1947.

Number.	Builder.	Laid dwn.	Launched.	Completed.
204.	See above list.	Unknown.	Unknown.	Unknown.

Fate: BU. 1948.

Number.	Builder.	Laid dwn.	Launched.	Completed.
070.	See above list.	Unknown.	Unknown.	Unknown.

Fate. Demolished on slipway. 1945.

Number.	Builder.	Laid dwn.	Launched.	Completed.
080.	See above list.	Unknown.	Unknown.	Unknown.

Fate. Demolished on slipway. 1945.

Number.	Builder.	Laid dwn.	Launched.	Completed.
112.	See above list.	Unknown.	Unknown.	Unknown.

Fate: Demolished on slipway. 1945.

MINELAYERS.

(Unclassed).
Displacement. 9,240 Tonnes. **Compliment:** Unknown.
Dimensions: 442'0" x 67'0" x 24'4".
Machinery: 2 Shaft Vte 1,800Ihp = 21.3Kts.
Fuel Cap: Unknown.
Armour: Belt-7.0" to 3.5", Deck-2.0", Turrets-6.0", Casemates-6.0"
Armament: 2 x 8.0", 8 x 6.0", 2 x 3.0", 1 x 3.0"AA, 300 Mines.
NB-: Launched as Armoured Cruiser. Much modified.
After 8.0" & Lower deck 6.0" Removed.
Armament became 4 x 6.0", 1 x 3.0"AA, 2 x 40mmAA, 35 x 25mmAA.

Name.	Builder.	Laid dwn.	Launched.	Completed.
TOKIWA.	Unknown.	Unknown.	1898.	Unknown.

Fate: Sunk. 08-08-45. At Ominato by US A/c. Salvaged & BU Postwar.

(Unclassed).
Displacement. 1,516 Tonnes. **Compliment:** Unknown.
Dimensions: 275'7" x 37'11" x 10'2".
Machinery: 2 Shaft Vte 2,000Ihp = 16.0Kts.
Fuel Cap: Unknown.
Armament: 3 x 4.7", 1 x MG, 100 Mines.

Name.	Builder.	Laid dwn.	Launched.	Completed.
SHIRATAKA.	Shikawajima Tokyo.	Unknown.	1929.	Unknown.

Fate: Sunk. 31-08-44. Torpedoed by US S/m.

Unclassed.
Displacement. 2,330 Tonnes. **Compliment:** 235.
Dimensions: 341'2" x 38'10" x 10'7".
Machinery: 3 Shaft Diesels, 3,000Bhp = 17.0Kts.
Fuel Cap: Unknown.
Armament: 3 x 5.5", 2 x 25mmAA, 6 x 13.2mmAA, 400 Mines.

Name.	Builder.	Laid dwn.	Launched.	Completed.
ITSUKUSHIMA.	Uraga Tokyo.	Unknown.	1929.	Unknown.

Fate: Sunk. 07-10-44. Torpedoed by Dutch S/m.

Unclassed.
Displacement. 1,358 Tonnes. **Compliment:** 150.
Dimensions: 292'0 x 34'11" x 9'4".
Machinery: 2 Shaft TE, 2 Boilers, 4,800Ihp = 20.0Kts.
Fuel Cap: Unknown.
Armament: 2 x 4.7", 2 x MG.AA, 185 Mines.
NB-: All refitted as escorts 1943-44. Minesweeping gear replaced by 36 DCs.

Name.	Builder.	Laid dwn.	Launched.	Completed.
YAEYAMA.	Kure Navy yd.	Unknown.	1931.	Unknown.

Fate: Sunk. 24-09-44. By US Carrier based A/c.

MINELAYERS.

Unclassed.

Displacement. 4,330 Tonnes.	Compliment: Unknown.

Dimensions: 408'6" x 51'3" x 16'2".
Machinery: 2 Shaft Geared Turbines, 4 Boilers, 9,000Shp = 20.0Kts.
Fuel Cap: Unknown.
Armament: 4 x 5.0", 4 x 25mmAA, 600 Mines, 1 x A/c.

Name.	Builder.	Laid dwn.	Launched.	Completed.
TSUGARU.	Yokosuka Navy yd.	Unknown.	1940.	Unknown.

Fate: Sunk. 29-06-44. Torpedoed by US S/m.

Unclassed.

Displacement. 574 Tonnes.	Compliment: Unknown.

Dimensions: 229'8" x 24'7" x 6'1".
Machinery: 2 Shaft Diesels, 2,100Bhp = 18.0Kts.
Fuel Cap: Unknown.
Armament: 2 x 3", 1 x 13.2mmAA, 120 Mines.

Name.	Builder.	Laid dwn.	Launched.	Completed.
SARUSHIMA.	Mitsibushi Yokohama.	Unknown.	1933.	Unknown.

Fate: Unknown..

Unclassed.

Displacement. 4,920 Tonnes.	Compliment: Unknown.

Dimensions: 391'4" x 51'8" x 18'0".
Machinery: 2 Shaft Geared Turbines, 9,000Shp = 20.0Kts.
Fuel Cap: Unknown.
Armament: 4 x 5.5", 2 x 3"AA, 500 Mines, 1 x A/c

Name.	Builder.	Laid dwn.	Launched.	Completed.
OKINOSHIMA.	Mitsibushi Yokohama.	Unknown.	1935.	Unknown.

Fate: Sunk. 11-05-42. Torpedoed by US S/m.

Unclassed.

Displacement. 738 Tonnes.	Compliment: 100.

Dimensions: 247'8" x 25'9" x 8'6".
Machinery: 2 Shaft Diesels, 3,500/3,600Bhp = 20.0Kts.
Fuel Cap: Unknown.
Armament: Main. Varied, 4 x 25mmAA, 600 Mines, 1 x A/c.

Name.	Builder.	Laid dwn.	Launched.	Completed.
SOKUTEN.	Mitsibushi Yokohama.	Unknown.	1939-43.	Unknown.

Fate: Sunk. 25-07-44. Cause unknown.

Name.	Builder.	Laid dwn.	Launched.	Completed.
SHIRIKAMA.	Ishikamajima Tokyo.	Unknown.	1939-43.	Unknown.

Fate: Sunk. 03-03-44. Cause unknown.

MINELAYERS. (Continued).

Unclassed.

Name.	Builder.	Laid dwn.	Launched.	Completed.
NARYU.	Mitsibushi Yokohama.	Unknown.	1939-43.	Unknown.

Fate: Sunk. 16-02-45. Cause unknown.

Name.	Builder.	Laid dwn.	Launched.	Completed.
KYOSAI.	Ishikawajima Tokyo.	Unknown.	1939-43.	Unknown.

Fate: To UK. 1947. BU.

Name.	Builder.	Laid dwn.	Launched.	Completed.
UKISHIMA.	Ishikamajima Tokyo.	Unknown.	1939-43.	Unknown.

Fate: Sunk. 16-11-43. Cause unknown.

Name.	Builder.	Laid dwn.	Launched.	Completed.
HARASHIMA.	Unknown.	Unknown.	1939-43.	Unknown.

Fate: Sunk. 27-07-43. Cause unknown.

Name.	Builder.	Laid dwn.	Launched.	Completed.
HOKO.	Unknown.	Unknown.	1939-43.	Unknown.

Fate: Sunk. 29-08-43. Cause unknown.

Name.	Builder.	Laid dwn.	Launched.	Completed.
ISHIKAZI.	Unknown.	Unknown.	1939-43.	Unknown.

Fate: To USA. 1947. BU.

Name.	Builder.	Laid dwn.	Launched.	Completed.
TAKASHIMA.	Unknown.	Unknown.	1939-43.	Unknown.

Fate: Lost. 10-10-44. Cause unknown.

Name.	Builder.	Laid dwn.	Launched.	Completed.
SAISHU.	Sasebo Navy yd.	Unknown.	1939-43.	Unknown.

Fate: To CHINA. 1947. Renamed YUNG CHING.

Name.	Builder.	Laid dwn.	Launched.	Completed.
NIIZAKI.	Unknown.	Unknown.	1939-43.	Unknown.

Fate: BU. 1947.

Name.	Builder.	Laid dwn.	Launched.	Completed.
YURIJIMA.	Unknown.	Unknown.	1939-43.	Unknown.

Fate: Sunk. 14-01-45. Cause unknown.

Name.	Builder.	Laid dwn.	Launched.	Completed.
NUWASHIMA.	Unknown.	Unknown.	1939-43.	Unknown.

Fate: BU. 1946.

Name.	Builder.	Laid dwn.	Launched.	Completed.
MAESHIMA.	C.T.L.	Unknown.	1939-43.	Unknown.

Fate: Sunk. 18-10-44. Cause unknown.

MINELAYERS. (Continued).

Unclassed. (Continued).

Name.	Builder.	Laid dwn.	Launched.	Completed.
AJIRO.	Hitachi Innoshima.	Unknown.	1939-43.	Unknown.

Fate: Sunk. 01-10-44. Cause unknown.

KAMOME. (Class).

Displacement. 502 Tonnes.   Compliment: 56.
Dimensions: 214'11 x 23'7" x 6'11".
Machinery: 2 Shaft TE, 2 Boilers, 2,500Ihp = 19.0Kts.
Fuel Cap: Unknown.
Armament: 1 x 3.0", 1 x 13.2mmAA, 120 Mines.
NB-: All refitted as escorts 1943-44. Minesweeping gear replaced by 36 DCs.

Name.	Builder.	Laid dwn.	Launched.	Completed.
KAMOME.	Osaka, Osaka.	Unknown.	1929.	Unknown.

Fate: Sunk. 27-04-44. Cause unknown.

Name.	Builder.	Laid dwn.	Launched.	Completed.
TSUBAME.	Mitsibushi Yokohama.	Unknown.	1929.	Unknown.

Fate: Sunk. 01-03-45. Cause unknown.

HATSUTAKA. Class.

Displacement. 1,860 Tonnes.   Compliment: Unknown.
Dimensions: 298'3" x 37'1" x 14'5".
Machinery: 2 Shaft Geared Turbines, 3 Boilers, 6,000Shp = 20.0Kts.
Fuel Cap: Unknown.
Armament: 4 x 40mmAA, 4 x 25mmAA, 360 Mines,
                 (WAKATAKE only 2 x 3.0"AA)

Name.	Builder.	Laid dwn.	Launched.	Completed.
HATSUTAKA.	Harima Aioi.	Unknown.	1939-44.	Unknown.

Fate: Sunk. 16-05-45. Cause unknown.

Name.	Builder.	Laid dwn.	Launched.	Completed.
AOTAKA.	Harima Aioi.	Unknown.	1939-44.	Unknown.

Fate: Sunk. 29-06-44. Cause unknown.

Name.	Builder.	Laid dwn.	Launched.	Completed.
WAKATAKE.	Harima Aioi.	Unknown.	1939-44.	Unknown.

Fate: To UK. 1947. Renamed HMS LABURNUM.

MINELAYERS. (Continued).

KAMISHIMA (Class).

Displacement. 787 Tonnes.		Compliment: Unknown.	
Dimensions:	244' 5" x 25'9" x 8'6".		
Machinery:	2 Shaft Diesels, 1,900Bhp = 16.5Kts.		
Fuel Cap:	Unknown.		
Armament:	2 x 40mmAA, 13 x 25mmAA, 120 Mines, 36 x DCs.		

Name.	Builder.	Laid dwn.	Launched.	Completed.
KAMISHIMA.	Sasebo Navy yd.	Unknown.	1945.	Unknown.

Fate: To USSR. 1947.

Name.	Builder.	Laid dwn.	Launched.	Completed.
AWASHIMA.	Sasebo Navy yd.	Unknown.	1945.	Unknown.

Fate: To USSR. 1947. BU.

HATSUSHIMA (Class).

Displacement. 1,670 Tonnes.		Compliment: Unknown.	
Dimensions:	262' 3" x 35'5" x 11'7".		
Machinery:	2 Shaft TE, 2 Boilers, 2,300Ihp = 14.0Kts.		
Fuel Cap:	Unknown.		
Armament:	1 x 3.0"AA, 2 x 13.2mmAA, 12 Mines.		

Name.	Builder.	Laid dwn.	Launched.	Completed.
HATSUSHIMA.	Kawasaki Kobe.	Unknown.	Unknown.	Unknown.

Fate: Sunk. 28-04-45. Cause unknown.

Name.	Builder.	Laid dwn.	Launched.	Completed.
TSURUSHIMA.	Kawasaki Kobe.	Unknown.	Unknown.	Unknown.

Fate: To Civilian use. 1945.

Name.	Builder.	Laid dwn.	Launched.	Completed.
ODATE.	Harima Harima.	Unknown.	Unknown.	Unknown.

Fate: Sunk. 27-03-45. Cause unknown.

Name.	Builder.	Laid dwn.	Launched.	Completed.
TATEISHI.	Harima Harima.	Unknown.	Unknown.	Unknown.

Fate: Sunk. 21-03-45. Cause unknown.

MINELAYERS. (Continued).

NASAME. (Class).

Displacement. 502 Tonnes. Compliment: Unknown.
Dimensions: 229'8" x 24'7" x 6'3".
Machinery: 2 Shaft Diesels, 2,300Bhp = 19.0Kts.
Fuel Cap: Unknown.
Armament: 2 x 3.0"AA, 2 x 13.2mmAA, 120 Mines.

Name.	Builder.	Laid dwn.	Launched.	Completed.
NASAME.	Kawasaki Kobe.	Unknown.	Unknown.	Unknown.

Fate: Sunk. 01-04-44. Cause unknown.

Name.	Builder.	Laid dwn.	Launched.	Completed.
NATSUSHIMA.	Ishikawajima Tokyo.	Unknown.	1933-34.	Unknown.

Fate: Sunk. 22-02-44. Cause unknown.

MINESWEEPERS.

W1. (Class).

Displacement. 691 Tonnes. Compliment: 92
Dimensions: 250' 2" x 26'4" x 7'6".
Machinery: 2 Shaft TE, 3 Boilers, 4,000Ihp = 20.0Kts.
Fuel Cap: Unknown.
Armament: 2 x 4.7", 1 x 3.0"AA.

Number.	Builder.	Laid dwn.	Launched.	Completed.
W.01.	Harima Harima.	Unknown.	1923-24.	Unknown.

Fate: Sunk. 10-08-45. Cause unknown.

Number.	Builder.	Laid dwn.	Launched.	Completed.
W.02.	Mitsui Tamano.	Unknown.	1923-24.	Unknown.

Fate: Sunk. 01-03-42. Cause unknown.

Number.	Builder.	Laid dwn.	Launched.	Completed.
W.03.	Hitachi Sakurajima.	Unknown.	1923-24.	Unknown.

Fate: Sunk. 09-04-45. Cause unknown.

Number.	Builder.	Laid dwn.	Launched.	Completed.
W.04.	Sasebo Navy yd.	Unknown.	1923-24.	Unknown.

Fate: Scuttled. 13-07-45.

W5. (Class).

Displacement. 691 Tonnes. Compliment: 92

Dimensions:	250' 2" x 26'4" x 7'6".
Machinery:	2 Shaft TE, 3 Boilers, 4,000Ihp = 20.0Kts.
Fuel Cap:	Unknown.
Armament:	2 x 4.7", 1 x 3.0"AA.

Number.	Builder.	Laid dwn.	Launched.	Completed.
W.05.	Harima Harima.	Unknown.	1928.	Unknown.

Fate: Sunk. 10-08-45. Cause unknown.

Number.	Builder.	Laid dwn.	Launched.	Completed.
W.06.	Mitsui Tamano.	Unknown.	1928.	Unknown.

Fate: Sunk. 01-03-42. Cause unknown.

MINESWEEPERS. (Continued).

W.13. (Class).

Displacement. 551 Tonnes. Compliment: Unknown.

Dimensions:	242' 9" x 26'11" x 6'9".
Machinery:	2 Shaft TE, 2 Boilers, 3,200Ihp = 20.0Kts.
Fuel Cap:	Unknown.
Armament:	2 x 4.7", 2 x 13.2mmAA.

Number.	Builder.	Laid dwn.	Launched.	Completed.
W.13.	Fujinagata Osaka.	Unknown.	1933-44.	Unknown.

Fate: Sunk. 12-01-42. Cause unknown.

Number.	Builder.	Laid dwn.	Launched.	Completed.
W.14.	Hitachi Sakurashima.	Unknown.	1933-44.	Unknown.

Fate: Sunk. 12-01-42. Cause unknown.

Number.	Builder.	Laid dwn.	Launched.	Completed.
W.15.	Fujinagata Osaka.	Unknown.	1933-44.	Unknown.

Fate: Sunk. 05-03-45. Cause unknown.

Number.	Builder.	Laid dwn.	Launched.	Completed.
W.16.	Mitsui Tamano.	Unknown.	1933-44.	Unknown.

Fate: Sunk. 11-09-43. Cause unknown.

W.17. (Class).

Displacement. 696 Tonnes. Compliment: Unknown.

Dimensions:	237'10" x 25'9" x 8'3".
Machinery:	2 Shaft Geared Turbines, 2 Boilers, 3,200Ihp = 19.0Kts.
Fuel Cap:	Unknown.
Armament:	2 x 4.7", 2 x 13.2mmAA.

Number.	Builder.	Laid dwn.	Launched.	Completed.
W.17.	Hitachi Sakurajima.	Unknown.	1935.	Unknown.

Fate: BU. 1947.

MINESWEEPERS. (Continued).

W.17. (Class). (Continued).

Number.	Builder.	Laid dwn.	Launched.	Completed.
W.18.	Mitsui Tamano.	Unknown.	1935.	Unknown

Fate: Sunk. 26-11-44. Cause unknown.

W.7. (Class).

Displacement. 738 Tonnes. Compliment: 88.
Dimensions: 237'10" x 25'9" x 6'7".
Machinery: 2 Shaft Geared Turbines, 2 Boilers, 3,850Shp = 20.0Kts.
Fuel Cap: Unknown.
Armament: 3 x 4.7", 2 x 13.2mmAA.

Number.	Builder.	Laid dwn.	Launched.	Completed.
W.07.	Mitsui Tamano.	Unknown.	1938-39.	Unknown.

Fate: Sunk. 15-04-44. Cause unknown.

Number.	Builder.	Laid dwn.	Launched.	Completed.
W.08:	Urago Tokyo.	Unknown.	1938-39.	Unknown.

Fate: Scuttled. 13-07-44.

Number.	Builder.	Laid dwn.	Launched.	Completed.
W.09.	Maizura Navy yd.	Unknown.	1938-39.	Unknown.

Fate: Sunk. 02-02-42. Cause unknown.

Number.	Builder.	Laid dwn.	Launched.	Completed.
W.10.	Ishikawajima Tokyo.	Unknown.	1938-39.	Unknown.

Fate. Sunk. 10-12-41. Cause unknown.

Number.	Builder.	Laid dwn.	Launched.	Completed.
W.11.	Uraga Tokyo.	Unknown.	1938-39.	Unknown.

Fate. Sunk. 28-03-45. Cause unknown.

Number.	Builder.	Laid dwn.	Launched.	Completed.
W.12.	Ishikawajima Tokyo.	Unknown.	1938-39.	Unknown.

Fate. Sunk. 06-04-45. Cause unknown.

W.19. Class.

Displacement. 738 Tonnes. Compliment: 88.
Dimensions: 237'10" x 25'9" x 6'7".
Machinery: 2 Shaft Geared Turbines, 2 Boilers, 3,850Shp = 20.0Kts.
Fuel Cap: Unknown.
Armament: 3 x 4.7", 2 x 13.2mmAA.

Number.	Builder.	Laid dwn.	Launched.	Completed.
W.19.	Unknown.	Unknown.	1941-44.	Unknown.

Fate: 10-12-41. Total constructional loss. Cause unknown.

MINESWEEPERS. (Continued).

W.19. (Class). (Continued).

Number.	Builder.	Laid dwn.	Launched.	Completed.
W.20.	Unknown.	Unknown.	1941-44.	Unknown.

Fate. Sunk. 04-05-45. Cause unknown.

Number.	Builder.	Laid dwn.	Launched.	Completed.
W.21.	Unknown.	Unknown.	1941-44.	Unknown.

Fate. To USA. 1947. BU.

Number.	Builder.	Laid dwn.	Launched.	Completed.
W.22.	Unknown.	Unknown.	1941-44.	Unknown.

Fate. Sunk. 11-11-44. Cause unknown.

Number.	Builder.	Laid dwn.	Launched.	Completed.
W.23.	Unknown.	Unknown.	1941-45.	Unknown.

Fate. To USSR. 1947.

Number.	Builder.	Laid dwn.	Launched.	Completed.
W.24.	Unknown.	Unknown.	1941-44.	Unknown.

Fate. Sunk. 15-07-45. Cause unknown.

Number.	Builder.	Laid dwn.	Launched.	Completed.
W.25.	Unknown.	Unknown.	1941-44.	Unknown.

Fate. Sunk. 04-07-44. Cause unknown.

Number.	Builder.	Laid dwn.	Launched.	Completed.
W.26.	Unknown.	Unknown.	1941-44.	Unknown.

Fate. Sunk. 17-02-44. Cause unknown.

Number.	Builder.	Laid dwn.	Launched.	Completed.
W.27.	Unknown.	Unknown.	1941-44.	Unknown.

Fate. Sunk. 10-07-45. Cause unknown.

Number.	Builder.	Laid dwn.	Launched.	Completed.
W.28.	Unknown.	Unknown.	1941-44.	Unknown.

Fate. Sunk. 29-08-44. Cause unknown.

Number.	Builder.	Laid dwn.	Launched.	Completed.
W.29.	Unknown.	Unknown.	1941-44.	Unknown.

Fate. Sunk. 07-05-45. Cause unknown.

Number.	Builder.	Laid dwn.	Launched.	Completed.
W.30.	Unknown.	Unknown.	1941-44.	Unknown.

Fate.Sunk. 11-11-44.

Number.	Builder.	Laid dwn.	Launched.	Completed.
W.33.	Unknown.	Unknown.	1941-44.	Unknown.

Fate. Sunk. 09-08-45. Cause.

MINESWEEPERS. (Continued).

W.19. (Class). (Continued).

Number.	Builder.	Laid dwn.	Launched.	Completed.
W.34.	Unknown.	Unknown.	1941-44.	Unknown

Fate. Sunk. 21-05-44. Cause unknown.

Number.	Builder.	Laid dwn.	Launched.	Completed.
W.38.	Unknown.	Unknown.	1941-44.	Unknown.

Fate. Sunk. 20-07-45. Cause unknown

Number.	Builder.	Laid dwn.	Launched.	Completed.
W.39.	Unknown.	Unknown.	1941-44.	Unknown.

Fate. Sunk. 20-07-45. Cause unknown.

Number.	Builder.	Laid dwn.	Launched.	Completed.
W.41.	Unknown.	Unknown.	1941-44.	Unknown.

Fate.Sunk. 04-01-45. Cause unknown.

SUBMARINE CHASERS.

CH. 1. (Class).

Displacement. 400 Tonnes.   Compliment: 45.
Dimensions: 210'0" x 19'4" x 4'8".
Machinery: Various, 3,400Bhp = 21.0Kts.
Fuel Cap: Unknown.
Armament: 2 x 40mmAA, 3 x 25.0mmAA, 1 x DCT, 36 DCs.

Number.	Builder.	Laid dwn.	Launched.	Completed.
CH.01.	Unknown.	Unknown.	1933-34.	Unknown.

Fate.Scuttled. Postwar.

Number.	Builder.	Laid dwn.	Launched.	Completed.
CH.02.	Unknown.	Unknown.	1935-36.	Unknown.

Fate. War loss. Cause unknown.

CH. 3. (Class).

Displacement. 280 Tonnes.   Compliment: 45.
Dimensions: 180'0" x 18'4" x 7'2"
Machinery: Various, 2 580Bhp = 20.0Kts.
Fuel Cap: Unknown.
Armament: 2 x 40mmAA, 3 x 25.0mmAA, 1 x DCT, 36 DCs.

Number.	Builder.	Laid dwn.	Launched.	Completed.
CH.03.	Unknown.	Unknown.	1939-42.	Unknown.

Fate. Scuttled. Post war.

Number.	Builder.	Laid dwn.	Launched.	Completed.
CH.04.	Unknown.	Unknown.	1939-42.	Unknown.

Fate. Scrapped. Post war.

SUB CHASERS.

CH. 3. (Class).

Number.	Builder.	Laid dwn.	Launched.	Completed.
CH.05.	Unknown.	Unknown.	1939-42.	Unknown.

Fate. Scuttled. Post war.

Number.	Builder.	Laid dwn.	Launched.	Completed.
CH.06.	Unknown.	Unknown.	1939-42.	Unknown.

Fate. War loss.

Number.	Builder.	Laid dwn.	Launched.	Completed.
CH.07.	Unknown.	Unknown.	1939-42.	Unknown.

Fate. War loss.

Number.	Builder.	Laid dwn.	Launched.	Completed.
CH.08.	Unknown.	Unknown.	1939-42.	Unknown.

Fate. War loss.

Number.	Builder.	Laid dwn.	Launched.	Completed.
CH.09.	Unknown.	Unknown.	1939-42.	Unknown.

Fate. To CHINA. 1947. Renamed FU LING.

Number.	Builder.	Laid dwn.	Launched.	Completed.
CH.10.	Unknown.	Unknown.	1939-42.	Unknown.

Fate. War loss.

Number.	Builder.	Laid dwn.	Launched.	Completed.
CH.11.	Unknown.	Unknown.	1939-42.	Unknown.

Fate. War loss.

Number.	Builder.	Laid dwn.	Launched.	Completed.
CH.12.	Unknown.	Unknown.	1939-42.	Unknown.

Fate. War loss.

Number.	Builder.	Laid dwn.	Launched.	Completed.
CH.13.	Unknown.	Unknown.	1939-42.	Unknown.

Fate. War loss.

Number.	Builder.	Laid dwn.	Launched.	Completed.
CH.14.	Unknown.	Unknown.	1939-42.	Unknown.

Fate: War loss.

Number.	Builder.	Laid dwn.	Launched.	Completed.
CH.15.	Unknown.	Unknown.	1939-42.	Unknown.

Fate: BU. Postwar.

Number.	Builder.	Laid dwn.	Launched.	Completed.
CH.16.	Unknown.	Unknown.	1939-42.	Unknown.

Fate: BU. Post war.

SUBMARINE CHASERS. (Continued).

CH.3. (Class). (Continued)

Number.	Builder.	Laid dwn.	Launched.	Completed.
CH.17.	Unknown.	Unknown.	1939-42.	Unknown,

Fate: BU. Post war.

Number.	Builder.	Laid dwn.	Launched.	Completed.
CH18..	Unknown.	Unknown.	1939-42.	Unknown.

Fate. War loss.

Number.	Builder.	Laid dwn.	Launched.	Completed.
CH.19.	Unknown.	Unknown.	1939-42.	Unknown.

Fate: BU. Post war.

Number.	Builder.	Laid dwn.	Launched.	Completed.
CH.20.	Unknown.	Unknown.	1939-42.	Unknown.

Fate: BU. Post war.

Number.	Builder.	Laid dwn.	Launched.	Completed.
CH.21.	Unknown.	Unknown.	1939-42.	Unknown.

Fate: BU. Post war.

Number.	Builder.	Laid dwn.	Launched.	Completed.
CH22.	Unknown.	Unknown.	1939-42.	Unknown.

Fate. War loss.

Number.	Builder.	Laid dwn.	Launched.	Completed.
CH.23.	Unknown.	Unknown.	1939-42.	Unknown.

Fate: BU. Post war.

Number.	Builder.	Laid dwn.	Launched.	Completed.
CH24.	Unknown.	Unknown.	1939-42.	Unknown.

Fate. War loss.

Number.	Builder.	Laid dwn.	Launched.	Completed.
CH25.	Unknown.	Unknown.	1939-42.	Unknown.

Fate. War loss.

Number.	Builder.	Laid dwn.	Launched.	Completed.
CH26.	Unknown.	Unknown.	1939-42.	Unknown.

Fate. War loss.

Number.	Builder.	Laid dwn.	Launched.	Completed.
CH27.	Unknown.	Unknown.	1939-42.	Unknown.

Fate. War loss.

SUBMARINE CHASERS. (Continued).

CH. 28. (Class).

Displacement. 435 Tonnes.		Compliment: Unknown.
Dimensions:	160'9" x 22'0" x 8'7"	
Machinery:	Various, 1'700Bhp = 16.0Kts.	
Fuel Cap:	Unknown.	
Armament:	1 x 3.0", 3 x 25mmAA, 2 x 13.2mmAA, 36 DCs.	

Number.	Builder.	Laid dwn.	Launched.	Completed.
CH.28.	Unknown.	Unknown.	1941-42.	Unknown.

Fate. To Russia. 1947.

Number.	Builder.	Laid dwn.	Launched.	Completed.
CH.29.	Unknown.	Unknown.	1941-42.	Unknown.

Fate: To CHINA. Renamed YA LUNG.

Number.	Builder.	Laid dwn.	Launched.	Completed.
CH.38.	Unknown.	Unknown.	1941-42.	Unknown.

Fate. Survived the war. No further information.

Number.	Builder.	Laid dwn.	Launched.	Completed.
CH.41.	Unknown.	Unknown.	1941-42.	Unknown.

Fate. Scuttled. Post war.

Number.	Builder.	Laid dwn.	Launched.	Completed.
CH.42.	Unknown.	Unknown.	1941-42.	Unknown

Fate. Survived the war. No further information.

Number.	Builder.	Laid dwn.	Launched.	Completed.
CH.44.	Unknown.	Unknown.	1941-42.	Unknown

Fate. Survived the war. No further information.

Number.	Builder.	Laid dwn.	Launched.	Completed.
CH.47.	Unknown.	Unknown.	1941-42.	Unknown

Fate. Survived the war. No further information.

Number.	Builder.	Laid dwn.	Launched.	Completed.
CH.49.	Unknown.	Unknown.	1941-42.	Unknown

Fate. Survived the war. No further information.

Number.	Builder.	Laid dwn.	Launched.	Completed.
CH.51.	Unknown.	Unknown.	1941-42.	Unknown

Fate. Sunk. During a storm.

Number.	Builder.	Laid dwn.	Launched.	Completed.
CH.52.	Unknown.	Unknown.	1941-42.	Unknown

Fate. Survived the war. No further information.

Number.	Builder.	Laid dwn.	Launched.	Completed.
CH.56.	Unknown.	Unknown.	1941-42.	Unknown

Fate. Survived the war. No further information.

MISCELLANEOUS VESSELS.

HASIDATE. (Class). (Gunboats).
Displacement. 1,092 Tonnes.   Compliment: 170.
Dimensions: 257'7" x 31'10" x 8'0"
Machinery: 2 Shaft, Geared Turbines, 2 Boilers. 4,660Shp = 19.5Kts.
Fuel Cap: Unknown.
Armament: 3 x 4.7", 9 x 25.0mmAA, Unknown amount of DCs.

Name.	Builder.	Laid dwn.	Launched.	Completed.
HASHIDATE.	Sakurajima Osaka.	Unknown.	1939-40.	Unknown.

Fate: Sunk. 22-05-44. Torpedoed by US S/m.

Name.	Builder.	Laid dwn.	Launched.	Completed.
UJI.	Sakurajima Osako.	Unknown.	1939-40.	Unknown.

Fate: To CHINA. 1945. Renamed CHANG CHI

ATAMI Class. (River Gunboats).
Displacement. 225 Tonnes.   Compliment: 77.
Dimensions: 184'7" x 20'8" x 3'0"
Machinery: 2 Shaft, TE, 2 Boilers. 1,300Ihp = 16.7Kts.
Fuel Cap: Unknown.
Armament: 1 x 3.0"AA, 5 x 25.0mmAA,

Name.	Builder.	Laid dwn.	Launched.	Completed.
ATAMI.	Fujinagata Osaka.	Unknown.	1929.	Unknown.

Fate: To CHINA. 1946. Renamed YUNG

Name.	Builder.	Laid dwn.	Launched.	Completed.
UJI.	Fujinagata Osako.	Unknown.	1929.	Unknown.

Fate: To CHINA. 1946. Renamed YUNG AN.

FUSHIMO (Class).
Displacement. 368 Tonnes.   Compliment: 64.
Dimensions: 164'0" x 32'2" x 4'2"
Machinery: 2 Shaft, Geared Turbines, 2 Boilers. 2,200Shp = 17.Kts.
Fuel Cap: Unknown.
Armament: 1 x 3.0"AA, 8 x 25.0mmAA,

Name.	Builder.	Laid dwn.	Launched.	Completed.
FUSHIMI.	Fujinagata Osaka.	Unknown.	1939.	Unknown.

Fate: To CHINA. 1946. Renamed KIANG HSI.

Name.	Builder.	Laid dwn.	Launched	Completed.
SUMIDA.	Fujinagata Osako.	Unknown.	1939.	Unknown.

Fate: To CHINA. 1946. Renamed NAN CHANG.

RIVER GUNBOATS. (Continued).

KOTAKA. (Class).

Displacement.	61.7 Tonnes.	Compliment: Unknown.
Dimensions:	100'1" x 32'2" x 4'2"	
Machinery:	2 Shaft, Diesels. 540Bhp = 15.5.Kts.	
Fuel Cap:	Unknown.	
Armament:	3 x 7.7mmAA.	

Name.	Builder.	Laid dwn.	Launched.	Completed.
TATRA.	Ex USN.	Unknown.	1930.	Unknown.

Fate: To CHINA. 1946. Renamed TAI YUAN.

Name.	Builder.	Laid dwn.	Launched.	Completed.
KARATSU.	Ex USN. (LUZON).	Unknown.	1930.	Unknown.

Fate: Scuttled. Off Manila. Before US Occupation.

Name.	Builder.	Laid dwn.	Launched.	Completed.
SUMA.	Ex BRITISH. (MOTH).	Unknown.	1930.	Unknown.

Fate: Mined. 19-03-45. Yangtse River.

Name.	Builder.	Laid dwn.	Launched.	Completed.
MAIKO.	Ex MACAU. (PORTU'SE	Unknown.	1930.	Unknown.

Fate: To CHINA. 1946. Renamed WU FENG.

Name.	Builder.	Laid dwn.	Launched.	Completed.
NARUMI.	Ex ITALIAN.	Unknown.	1930.	Unknown.

Fate: To CHINA. 1946. Renamed KIANG KUN.

COASTAL ESCORTS.

TYPE A.

Displacement.	277 Tonnes.	Compliment: Unknown.
Dimensions:	159'1" x 17'9" x 7'9"	
Machinery:	Various. 800Bhp = 15.0.Kts.	
Fuel Cap:	Unknown.	
Armament:	1 x 40mmAA, 6 x 25mmAA, 60 x DCs.	
	Or 1 Kaiten, 8 x DCs.	

NB:- ALTHOUGH LAUNCHED NEVER COMPLETED.

COASTAL ESCORTS.

TYPE B.

Displacement.	285 Tonnes.	Compliment: Unknown.
Dimensions:	123'0" x 20'0" x 8'0"	
Machinery:	Various. 800Bhp = 15.0.Kts.	
Fuel Cap:	Unknown.	
Armament:	1 x 40mmAA, 6 x 25mmAA, 60 x DCs.	
	Or 1 Kaiten, 8 x DCs.	

NB:- 101 to 157 LAID DOWN NEVER LAUNCHED.

SURVEY SHIP.

Displacement. 1,575 Tonnes.   Compliment: Unknown.
Dimensions: 172'4" x 34'9" x 11'10"
Machinery: 3 Shaft Diesels, 5,700Bhp = 19.7.Kts.
Fuel Cap: Unknown.
Armament: 4 x 4.7"AA, 1 x A/c.

Name.	Builder.	Laid dwn.	Launched.	Completed.
TSUKUSHI.	Mitsibushi Yokohama.	Unknown.	1941.	Unknown.

Fate: Sunk. 04-11-43. Mined.

SEAPLANE CARRIER.

Displacement. 14,050 Tonnes.   Compliment: 155.
Dimensions: 455'8" x 58'0" x 26'6"
Machinery: 2 Shaft TE, 4 Boilers, 5,850Bhp = 12.0.Kts.
Fuel Cap: Unknown.
Armament: 2 x 4.7", 2x 3.0"AA, 10 x A/c.

Name.	Builder.	Laid dwn.	Launched.	Completed.
NOTORO.	Kawasaki Kobe.	Unknown.	03-05-20.	Unknown.

Fate: BU. 1947.

SEAPLANE CARRIER.

Displacement. 14,050 Tonnes.   Compliment: 155.
Dimensions: 455'8" x 58'0" x 26'6"
Machinery: 2 Shaft TE, 4 Boilers, 5,850Bhp = 12.0.Kts.
Fuel Cap: Unknown.
Armament: 2 x 4.7", 2x 3.0"AA, 10 x A/c.

Name.	Builder.	Laid dwn.	Launched.	Completed.
KAMOI.	New York Co Camden.	Unknown.	08-06-38.	Unknown.

Fate: Sunk. 05-04-45. US A/c Hong at Kong.

SEAPLANE CARRIER.

CHITOISE. (Class).
Displacement. 11,023 Tonnes.   Compliment: Unknown.
Dimensions: 603'4" x 61'8" x 23'8"
Machinery: 2 Shaft Geared Turbines, 4 Boilers, 44,000Shp = 12.0.Kts.
                         Diesel Motors, 12,800Bhp
Fuel Cap: Unknown.
Armament: 4 x 5.0", 12 x 25mmAA, 24 x A/c.

Name.	Builder.	Laid dwn.	Launched.	Completed.
CHITOISE.	Kure Navy yd.	Unknown.	29-11-36.	Unknown.

Fate: Unknown.

SEAPLANE CARRIER. (Continued).

CHITOISE. (Class). (Continued).

Name.	Builder.	Laid dwn.	Launched.	Completed.
CHYODA.	Kure Navy yd.	Unknown.	19-11-37.	Unknown.

Complement: Unknown.

Fate: Unknown..

SEAPLANE CARRIER.

MIZUHO. (Class).
Displacement. 11,960 Tonnes. Compliment: Unknown.
Dimensions: 602'4" x 61'8" x 23'3"
Machinery: 2 Shaft Diesels. 15,200Bhp = 22.0.Kts.
Fuel Cap: Unknown.
Armament: 6 x 5.0", 12 x 25mmAA, 24 x A/c.

Name.	Builder.	Laid dwn.	Launched.	Completed.
MIZUHO.	Kawasaki Kobe.	Unknown.	16-05-38.	Unknown.

Fate: Sunk. 02-05-42. Torpedoed by US S/m.

SEAPLANE CARRIER.

NISSHIN. (Class).
Displacement. 12,300 Tonnes. Compliment: Unknown.
Dimensions: 616'10" x 64'8" x 23'0"
Machinery: 2 Shaft Diesels 47,000Bhp = 22.0.Kts.
Fuel Cap: Unknown.
Armament: 6 x 5.5", 18 x 25mmAA, 20 x A/c.

Name.	Builder.	Laid dwn.	Launched.	Completed.
NISSHIN.	Kure Navy yd.	Unknown.	30-11-39.	Unknown.

Fate: Sunk. 22-07-43. By US A/c S/West Pacific Area.

MERCHANT SHIPS. converted into SEAPLANE CARRIERS.
Displacement: Unknown. Compliment: Unknown.
Dimensions: Unknown.
Machinery: Unknown..
Fuel Cap: Unknown.
Armament: 2 x 6.0" (1 on the Bow & 1 on the Stern), 2 x 13.2mmAA.
NB:-NEVER CONVERTED INTO SEAPLANE CARRIERS.
REVERTED BACK TO TRANSPORTS.

KAGA MARU.
KINUGASA MARU.
KYOKAWA MARU.
KUNIKAWA MARU.
SAGARA MARU.
SANUKI MARU.
SANYO MARU.
KAMIKAWA MARU. Sunk. May 1943. No further information available.

FLYING BOAT TENDER.

Displacement. 4,900 Tonnes.   Compliment: Unknown.
Dimensions: 387'0" x 51'10" x 17'9"
Machinery: 2 Shaft Diesels. 8,000Bhp = 19,0,Kts.
Fuel Cap: Unknown.
Armament: 4 x 5.0", 10 x 25mmAA, 1 x Large Flying Boat.

Name.	Builder.	Laid dwn.	Launched.	Completed.
AKITSUSHIMA.	Unknown.	Unknown.	1941.	Unknown.

Fate: Sunk. 24-09-44. By US Carrier Based A/c.

AIRCRAFT TRANSPORT.

SHIMANE MARU. (Class).
Displacement. 14,270 Tonnes.   Compliment: Unknown.
Dimensions: 526'7" x 65'7" x 29'10"
Machinery: 1 Shaft, Geared Turbines, 2 Boilers. 8,600Shp = 18.0.Kts.
Fuel Cap: Unknown.
Armament: 2 x 4.7", 52 x 25mmAA, 12 x A/c. 10 x DCs.

Name.	Builder.	Laid dwn.	Launched.	Completed.
SHIMANE.	Unknown.	Unknown.	1944-45.	Unknown.

Fate: Sunk. 24-07-45. By US Carrier Based A/c.

Name.	Builder.	Laid dwn.	Launched.	Completed.
OTAKISAN.	Unknown.	Unknown.	1944-45.	Unknown.

Fate: Sunk. 24-07-45. Mined.

AIRCRAFT TRANSPORT.

YAMASHIRO MARU. (Class).
Displacement. 15,613 Tonnes.   Compliment: 221.
Dimensions: 516'6" x 66'11" x 29'6"
Machinery: 1 Shaft, Geared Turbines, 2 Boilers. 4,500Shp = 15.0.Kts.
Fuel Cap: Unknown.
Armament: 16 x 25mmAA, 8 x A/c. 120 x DCs.

Name.	Builder.	Laid dwn.	Launched.	Completed.
YAMISHIRO.	Mitsibushi Yokohama.	Unknown.	1944.	Unknown.

Fate: Sunk. 17-02-45. By US A/c.

Name.	Builder.	Laid dwn.	Launched.	Completed.
CHIGUSA.	Yokohama Yokohama.	Unknown.	1944.	Unknown.

Fate: Completed into Civillian use.

LANDING SHIP. (With Flight Deck).

AKITSU MARU. (Class).
Displacement. 15,613 Tonnes.   Compliment: 221.
Dimensions: 516'6" x 66'11" x 29'6"
Machinery: 1 Shaft, Geared Turbines, 4 Boilers. 7,500Shp = 20.0.Kts.
Fuel Cap: Unknown.
Armament: 2 x 3.0"AA, 10 x 3.0" (Field guns), 20 x A/c.

Name.	Builder.	Laid dwn.	Launched.	Completed.
AKITSU.	Harima Harima.	Unknown.	1941-42.	Unknown.

Fate: Sunk. 15-11-44. Torpedoed by US S/m.

Name.	Builder.	Laid dwn.	Launched.	Completed.
NIGITSU.	Harima Harima.	Unknown.	1941-42.	Unknown.

Fate: Sunk. 12-01-44. Torpedoed by US S/m.

LANDING SHIP. (With Flight Deck).

KUMANO MARU. (Class).
Displacement. 11,800 Tonnes.   Compliment: Unknown..
Dimensions: 501'0" x 64'3" x 23'0"
Machinery: 2 Shaft, Geared Turbines, 4 Boilers. 1'000Shp = 19.0.Kts.
Fuel Cap: Unknown.
Armament: 8 x 3.0"AA, 6 x 25mmAA, 8-37 x A/c.

Name.	Builder.	Laid dwn.	Launched.	Completed.
KUMANO.	Unknown.	Unknown.	Unknown.	Unknown.

Fate: Reverted to Civillian use Post war.

LANDING SHIP.

SHINSHU MARU. (Class).
Displacement. 11,800 Tonnes.   Compliment: Unknown..
Dimensions: 492'2" x 72'2" x 26'9"
Machinery: 2 Shaft, Geared Turbines. 8,000Shp = 19.0.Kts.
Fuel Cap: Unknown.
Armament: 8 x 3.0"AA, 20-37 x A/c.
NB:- First purpose built Landing Craft.
      Capable of exiting 20 landing craft through stern doors.

Name.	Builder.	Laid dwn.	Launched.	Completed.
SHINSHU.	Unknown.	Unknown.	Unknown.	Unknown.

Fate: Sunk. By stray Japanese torpedo. Java Landings.
      Salvaged & Repaired 1943.
      Sunk. 05-01-45. By US A/c off Formosa.

LANDING SHIPS. (Continued).

T.1. (Class).
Displacement. 1,770 Tonnes.   **Compliment:** Unknown..
Dimensions: 315'0" x 33'5" x 11'10"
Machinery: 1 Shaft, Geared Turbines, 2 Boilers,   9,500Shp = 22.0.Kts.
Fuel Cap: Unknown.
Armament: 2 x 5.0", 26 x 25.0mmAA, 42 x DCs.

Number.	Builder.	Laid dwn.	Launched.	Completed.
T.01.	Unknown.	Unknown.	1944-45.	Unknown.

Fate. Sunk. 27-07-44. Cause unknown.

Number.	Builder.	Laid dwn.	Launched.	Completed.
T.02.	Unknown.	Unknown.	1944-45.	Unknown.

Fate. Sunk. 05-08-44. Cause unknown.

Number.	Builder.	Laid dwn.	Launched.	Completed.
T.03.	Unknown.	Unknown.	1944-45.	Unknown.

Fate. Sunk. 14-09-44. Cause unknown.

Number.	Builder.	Laid dwn.	Launched.	Completed.
T.04.	Unknown.	Unknown.	1944-45.	Unknown.

Fate. Sunk. 04-08-44. Cause unknown.

Number.	Builder.	Laid dwn.	Launched.	Completed.
T.05.	Unknown.	Unknown.	1944-45.	Unknown.

Fate. Sunk. 14-09-44. Cause unknown.

Number.	Builder.	Laid dwn.	Launched.	Completed.
T.06.	Unknown.	Unknown.	1944-45.	Unknown.

Fate. Sunk. 25-11`-44. Cause unknown.

Number.	Builder.	Laid dwn.	Launched.	Completed.
T.07.	Unknown.	Unknown.	1944-45.	Unknown.

Fate. Sunk. 27-12-44. Cause unknown.

Number.	Builder.	Laid dwn.	Launched.	Completed.
T.08.	Unknown.	Unknown.	1944-45.	Unknown.

Fate. Sunk. 24-12-44. Cause unknown.

Number.	Builder.	Laid dwn.	Launched.	Completed.
T.09.	Unknown.	Unknown.	1944-45.	Unknown.

Fate. To USA. 1947. BU.

Number.	Builder.	Laid dwn.	Launched.	Completed.
T.10.	Unknown.	Unknown.	1944-45.	Unknown.

Fate. Sunk. 25-11`-44. Cause unknown.

Number.	Builder.	Laid dwn.	Launched.	Completed.
T.11.	Unknown.	Unknown.	1944-45.	Unknown.

Fate. Sunk. 07-12-44. Cause unknown.

LANDING SHIPS. (Continued).

T.1. (Class). (Continued).

Number.	Builder.	Laid dwn.	Launched.	Completed.
T.12.	Unknown.	Unknown.	1944-45.	Unknown.

Fate. Sunk. 13-12-44.

Number.	Builder.	Laid dwn.	Launched.	Completed.
T.13.	Unknown.	Unknown.	1944-45.	Unknown.

Fate. Sunk. 25-11-44. Cause unknown.

Number.	Builder.	Laid dwn.	Launched.	Completed.
T.11.	Unknown.	Unknown.	1944-45.	Unknown.

Fate. 07-12`-44. Cause unknown.

Number.	Builder.	Laid dwn.	Launched.	Completed.
T.12.	Unknown.	Unknown.	1944-45.	Unknown.

Fate. Sunk. 13-12-44. Cause unknown.

Number.	Builder.	Laid dwn.	Launched.	Completed.
T.13.	Unknown.	Unknown.	1944-45.	Unknown.

Fate. To USSR. 1947. BU.

Number.	Builder.	Laid dwn.	Launched.	Completed.
T.14.	Unknown.	Unknown.	1944-45.	Unknown.

Fate. Sunk. 15-01-45. Cause unknown.

Number.	Builder.	Laid dwn.	Launched.	Completed.
T.15.	Unknown.	Unknown.	1944-45.	Unknown.

Fate. Sunk. 17-01-45. Cause unknown.

Number.	Builder.	Laid dwn.	Launched.	Completed.
T.16.	Unknown.	Unknown.	1944-45.	Unknown.

Fate. To CHINA. 1947. Renamed WU I.

Number.	Builder.	Laid dwn.	Launched.	Completed.
T.17.	Unknown.	Unknown.	1944-45.	Unknown.

Fate. Sunk. 02-04-45. Cause unknown.

Number.	Builder.	Laid dwn.	Launched.	Completed.
T.18.	Unknown.	Unknown.	1944-45.	Unknown.

Fate. Sunk. After 18-03-45. Cause unknown.

Number.	Builder.	Laid dwn.	Launched.	Completed.
T.19.	Unknown.	Unknown.	1944-45.	Unknown.

Fate. To UK. 1947. BU.

Number.	Builder.	Laid dwn.	Launched.	Completed.
T.20.	Unknown.	Unknown.	1944-45.	Unknown.

Fate. Lost Post war. 25-09-46.

LANDING SHIPS. (Continued)

T.1. Class. (Continued).

Number.	Builder.	Laid dwn.	Launched.	Completed.
T.21.	Unknown.	Unknown.	1944-45.	Unknown.

Fate. Sunk. 10-08-45. Cause unknown.

T.101. Class.

Displacement. 994 Tonnes.   Compliment: 90.
Dimensions: 264'0" x 29'10" x 9'6"
Machinery: 3 Shaft Diesels, 1,200Bhp = 13.5.Kts.
Fuel Cap: Unknown.
Armament: 1 x 3.0"AA, 21 x 25.0mmAA, 12 x DCs.

Number.	Builder.	Laid dwn.	Launched.	Completed.
T.101.	Unknown.	Unknown.	1944.	Unknown.

Fate. Sunk. 28-10-44. Cause unknown.

Number.	Builder.	Laid dwn.	Launched.	Completed.
T.102.	Unknown.	Unknown.	1944.	Unknown.

Fate. Sunk. 26-10-44. Cause unknown.

Number.	Builder.	Laid dwn.	Launched.	Completed.
T.108.	Unknown.	Unknown.	1944.	Unknown.

Fate. Sunk. 04-06-44. Cause unknown.

Number.	Builder.	Laid dwn.	Launched.	Completed.
T.127.	Unknown.	Unknown.	1944.	Unknown.

Fate. Sunk. 24-09-44. Cause unknown.

Number.	Builder.	Laid dwn.	Launched.	Completed.
T.149.	Unknown.	Unknown.	1944.	Unknown.

Fate. Sunk. 12-01-45. Constructional loss. BU 1946.

Number.	Builder.	Laid dwn.	Launched.	Completed.
T.150.	Unknown.	Unknown.	1944.	Unknown.

Fate. Sunk. 04-06-44. Cause unknown.

LANDING SHIPS. (Continued).

T.103. (Class).
Displacement. 994 Tonnes.   Compliment: 90.
Dimensions: 264'0" x 29'10" x 9'6"
Machinery: 3 Shaft Diesels, 1200Bhp = 13.5.Kts.
Fuel Cap: Unknown.
Armament: 1 x 3.0"AA, 21 x 25.0mmAA, 12 x DCs.

Number.	Builder.	Laid dwn.	Launched.	Completed.
T.103.	Unknown.	Unknown.	1944-45.	Unknown.

Fate: Sunk. 04-07-44. Cause unknown.

Number.	Builder.	Laid dwn.	Launched.	Completed.
T.104.	Unknown.	Unknown.	1944-45.	Unknown.

Fate: Sunk. 13-12-44. Cause unknown.

Number.	Builder.	Laid dwn.	Launched.	Completed.
T.105.	Unknown.	Unknown.	1944-45.	Unknown.

Fate: Sunk. 11-10-44. Cause unknown.

Number.	Builder.	Laid dwn.	Launched.	Completed.
T.106.	Unknown.	Unknown.	1944-45.	Unknown.

Fate: Sunk. 15-12-44. Cause unknown.

Number.	Builder.	Laid dwn.	Launched.	Completed.
T.107.	Unknown.	Unknown.	1944-45.	Unknown.

Fate: Sunk. 05-01-45. Cause unknown.

Number.	Builder.	Laid dwn.	Launched.	Completed.
T.108:	Unknown.	Unknown.	1944-45.	Unknown.

Fate: BU. 1946.

Number.	Builder.	Laid dwn.	Launched.	Completed.
T.111.	Unknown.	Unknown.	1944-45.	Unknown.

Fate: Sunk. 24-11-44. Cause unknown.

Number.	Builder.	Laid dwn.	Launched.	Completed.
T.112.	Unknown.	Unknown.	1944-45.	Unknown.

Fate: Sunk. 05-11-44. Cause unknown.

Number.	Builder.	Laid dwn.	Launched.	Completed.
T113.	Unknown.	Unknown.	1944-45.	Unknown.

Fate: Sunk. 25-11-44. Cause unknown

Number.	Builder.	Laid dwn.	Launched.	Completed.
T.114.	Unknown.	Unknown.	1944-45.	Unknown.

Fate: Sunk. 17-02-45. Cause unknown.

LANDING SHIPS. (Continued).

T.103. (Class). (Continued).

Number.	Builder.	Laid dwn.	Launched.	Completed.
T.129.	Unknown.	Unknown.	1944-45.	Unknown.

Fate: Sunk. 14-08-44. Cause unknown.

Number.	Builder.	Laid dwn.	Launched.	Completed.
T.130.	Unknown.	Unknown.	1944-45.	Unknown.

Fate: Sunk. 04-07-44. Cause unknown.

Number.	Builder.	Laid dwn.	Launched.	Completed.
T.132.	Unknown.	Unknown.	1944-45.	Unknown.

Fate: Sunk. 27-12-44. Cause unknown.

Number.	Builder.	Laid dwn.	Launched.	Completed.
T.133.	Unknown.	Unknown.	1944-45.	Unknown.

Fate: Sunk. 04-08-44. Cause unknown.

Number.	Builder.	Laid dwn.	Launched.	Completed.
T.134.	Unknown.	Unknown.	1944-45.	Unknown.

Fate: Sunk. 04-10-44. Cause unknown.

Number.	Builder.	Laid dwn.	Launched.	Completed.
T.135.	Unknown.	Unknown.	1944-45.	Unknown.

Fate: Sunk. 18-10-44. Cause unknown.

Number.	Builder.	Laid dwn.	Launched.	Completed.
T.136.	Unknown.	Unknown.	1944-45.	Unknown.

Fate: Sunk. 18-10-44. Cause unknown.

Number.	Builder.	Laid dwn.	Launched.	Completed.
T.138.	Unknown.	Unknown.	1944-45.	Unknown.

Fate: Sunk. 26-10-44. Cause unknown.

Number.	Builder.	Laid dwn.	Launched.	Completed.
T.139.	Unknown.	Unknown.	1944-45.	Unknown.

Fate: Sunk. 06-11-44. Cause unknown.

Number.	Builder.	Laid dwn.	Launched.	Completed.
T.140.	Unknown.	Unknown.	1944-45.	Unknown.

Fate: Sunk. 12-01-45. Cause unknown.

Number.	Builder.	Laid dwn.	Launched.	Completed.
T.141.	Unknown.	Unknown.	1944-45.	Unknown.

Fate: Sunk. 25-11-45. Cause unknown.

Number.	Builder.	Laid dwn.	Launched.	Completed.
T.142.	Unknown.	Unknown.	1944-45.	Unknown.

Fate: Sunk. 25-11-44. Cause unknown.

LANDING SHIPS. (Continued).

T.103. (Class). (Continued).

Number.	Builder.	Laid dwn.	Launched.	Completed.
T.143.	Unknown.	Unknown.	1944-45.	Unknown.

Fate: Sunk. 08-02-45. Cause unknown.

Number.	Builder.	Laid dwn.	Launched.	Completed.
T.146.	Unknown.	Unknown.	1944-45.	Unknown.

Fate: Sunk. 28-04-45. Cause unknown.

Number.	Builder.	Laid dwn.	Launched.	Completed.
T.147.	Unknown.	Unknown.	1944-45.	Unknown.

Fate: To UK. 1947. BU.

Number.	Builder.	Laid dwn.	Launched.	Completed.
T.151.	Unknown.	Unknown.	1944-45.	Unknown.

Fate: Sunk. 23-11-44. Cause unknown.

Number.	Builder.	Laid dwn.	Launched.	Completed.
T.152.	Unknown.	Unknown.	1944-45.	Unknown.

Fate: Sunk. 02-08-44. Cause unknown.

Number.	Builder.	Laid dwn.	Launched.	Completed.
T.153.	Unknown.	Unknown.	1944-45.	Unknown.

Fate: To UK. 1947. BU.

Number.	Builder.	Laid dwn.	Launched.	Completed.
T.154.	Unknown.	Unknown.	1944-45.	Unknown.

Fate: Sunk. 05-01-45. Cause unknown.

Number.	Builder.	Laid dwn.	Launched.	Completed.
T.157.	Unknown.	Unknown.	1944-45.	Unknown.

Fate: Sunk. 24-12-44. Cause unknown.

Number.	Builder.	Laid dwn.	Launched.	Completed.
T.158.	Unknown.	Unknown.	1944-45.	Unknown.

Fate: Sunk. 10-10-44. Cause unknown.

Number.	Builder.	Laid dwn.	Launched.	Completed.
T.159.	Unknown.	Unknown.	1944-45.	Unknown.

Fate: Sunk. 12-12-44. Cause unknown.

Number.	Builder.	Laid dwn.	Launched.	Completed.
T.160.	Unknown.	Unknown.	1944-45.	Unknown.

Fate: Sunk. 24-11-44. Cause unknown.

Number.	Builder.	Laid dwn.	Launched.	Completed.
T.161.	Unknown.	Unknown.	1944-45.	Unknown.

Fate: Sunk. 25-11-44. Cause unknown.

LANDING SHIPS. (Continued).

T.103. (Class). (Continued).

Number.	Builder.	Laid dwn.	Launched.	Completed.
T.173.	Unknown.	Unknown.	1944-45.	Unknown.

Fate: Sunk. 22-05-45. Cause unknown.

Number.	Builder.	Laid dwn.	Launched.	Completed.
T.174.	Unknown.	Unknown.	1944-45.	Unknown.

Fate: To USA. 1948. BU.

SS. Class.

Displacement. 933 Tonnes.   Compliment: Unknown..
Dimensions: 206'9" x 31'6" x 9'2"
Machinery: 2 Shaft Diesels, 1,100Bhp = 13.5.Kts.
Fuel Cap: Unknown.
Armament: 1 x 3.0"AA, 4 x 20.0mmAA, 4 x 7.7mmAA, 1 x Mortar.

Number.	Builder.	Laid dwn.	Launched.	Completed.
SS. 01.	Unknown.	Unknown.	1942-44.	Unknown.

Fate: Sunk. 13-01-45. Cause unknown.

Number.	Builder.	Laid dwn.	Launched.	Completed.
SS.02.	Unknown.	Unknown.	1942-44.	Unknown.

Fate: Sunk. 27-03-44. Cause unknown.

Number.	Builder.	Laid dwn.	Launched.	Completed.
SS.03.	Unknown.	Unknown.	1942-44.	Unknown.

Fate: Sunk. 28-10-44. Cause unknown.

Number.	Builder.	Laid dwn.	Launched.	Completed.
SS.04.	Unknown.	Unknown.	1942-44.	Unknown.

Fate: Sunk. 1944. Cause unknown.

Number.	Builder.	Laid dwn.	Launched.	Completed.
SS.05.	Unknown.	Unknown.	1942-44.	Unknown.

Fate: Sunk. 30-11-44. Cause unknown.

Number.	Builder.	Laid dwn.	Launched.	Completed.
SS.06.	Unknown.	Unknown.	1942-44.	Unknown.

Fate: Sunk. 04-12-44. Cause unknown.

Number.	Builder.	Laid dwn.	Launched.	Completed.
SS.07.	Unknown.	Unknown.	Unknown.	Unknown.

Fate: Sunk. 04-12-44. Cause unknown.

Number.	Builder.	Laid dwn.	Launched.	Completed.
SS.08.	Unknown.	Unknown.	Unknown.	Unknown.

Fate: Sunk. 04-12-44. Cause unknown.

LANDING SHIPS. (Continued).

SS. Class. (Continued).

Number.	Builder.	Laid dwn.	Launched.	Completed.
SS.09.	Unknown.	Unknown.	1942-44.	Unknown.

Fate. Sunk. 28-10-44. Cause unknown.

Number.	Builder.	Laid dwn.	Launched.	Completed.
SS.10.	Unknown.	Unknown.	1942-44.	Unknown.

Fate: Sunk. 1945. Cause unknown.

Number.	Builder.	Laid dwn.	Launched.	Completed.
SS.11.	Unknown.	Unknown.	1942-44.	Unknown.

Fate: Sunk. 1945. Cause unknown.

Number.	Builder.	Laid dwn.	Launched.	Completed.
SS.12.	Unknown.	Unknown.	1942-44.	Unknown.

Fate: BU. 1945.

Number.	Builder.	Laid dwn.	Launched.	Completed.
SS.13.	Unknown.	Unknown.	1942-44.	Unknown.

Fate: BU. 1945-46.

Number.	Builder.	Laid dwn.	Launched.	Completed.
SS.14.	Unknown.	Unknown.	1942-44.	Unknown.

Fate: Sunk. 05-06-45. Cause unknown.

Number.	Builder.	Laid dwn.	Launched.	Completed.
SS.15.	Unknown.	Unknown.	1942-44.	Unknown.

Fate: Sunk. 28-10-44. Cause unknown.

Number.	Builder.	Laid dwn.	Launched.	Completed.
SS.21.	Unknown.	Unknown.	1942-44.	Unknown.

Fate: Sunk. 01-06-45. Cause unknown.

LANDING SHIPS.

Displacement. 21.4 Tonnes.   Compliment: 12.
Dimensions: 47'11" x 11'0" x 2'6"
Machinery: Various, 150Bhp = 8.5.Kts.
Fuel Cap: Unknown.
Armament: 2 x 25.0mmAA, 2 x 7.7mmAA, 4 x DCs.

Type.	Naval.	Army.	No Built.
10.M.	Shohatsu.	SB-C.	20.
13.M.	Chuhatsu.	------	3.
15.M.	Moko Diahatsu.	------	1140.
17.M.	Toko Diahatsu.	------	163.

MOTOR TORPEDO BOAT.
19 METRE Type.

Displacement. 18.7 Tonnes.   Compliment: Unknown.
Dimensions: 62'4" x 14'1" x 3'11"
Machinery: Various, 1860Bhp = 35.0.Kts.
Fuel Cap: Unknown.
Armament: 2 x 18" Torpedo's, 2 x 17.7mmAA.

Number.	Builder.	Laid dwn.	Launched.	Completed.
T.A1.	Unknown.	Unknown.	1940.	Unknown.

Fate: Sunk. 28-10-44. Cause unknown.

T.1. Type.

Displacement. 20.5 Tonnes.   Compliment: Unknown.
Dimensions: 60'0" x 14'1" x 2'2"
Machinery: Various, 1860Bhp = 38.5.Kts.
Fuel Cap: Unknown.
Armament: 2 x 18" Torpedo's, 2 x 17.7mmAA., 6 x DCs.

Number.	Builder.	Laid dwn.	Launched.	Completed.
T.01.	Unknown.	Unknown.	1943-45.	Unknown.

Fate: Scrapped. Post war.

Number.	Builder.	Laid dwn.	Launched.	Completed.
T.02.	Unknown.	Unknown.	1943-45.	Unknown.

Fate: Sunk. War loss. Cause & Date unknown.

Number.	Builder.	Laid dwn.	Launched.	Completed.
T.03.	Unknown.	Unknown.	1943-45.	Unknown.

Fate: Cause & Date unknown.

Number.	Builder.	Laid dwn.	Launched.	Completed.
T.04.	Unknown.	Unknown.	1943-45.	Unknown.

Fate: Cause & Date unknown.

Number.	Builder.	Laid dwn.	Launched.	Completed.
T.05.	Unknown.	Unknown.	1943-45.	Unknown.

Fate: Cause & Date unknown.

Number.	Builder.	Laid dwn.	Launched.	Completed.
T.06.	Unknown.	Unknown.	1943-45.	Unknown.

Fate: Sunk. War loss. Cause & Date unknown.

MOTOR TORPEDO BOAT. (Continued).
T.23. T.25. T.31. T.39. Type.

Displacement. 25.0 Tonnes.   Compliment: 7.
Dimensions: 59'1" x 14'1" x 2'5"
Machinery: Various,
Fuel Cap: Unknown.
Armament: 2 x 18" Torpedo's, 1 x 25.0mmAA or 1 x 13.2mmAA, 6 x DCs.

T.23. 201, 207, 401, 410, 451, 456.

T.25. 468, 484, 488.

T.31. 208, 240.

T.32. 301, 308.

T.33. 500, 505.

T.34. 151, 165.

T.35. 469, 482, 483, 494, 499, 529, 537, 801, 937.

T.36. 411, 450, 470, 473.

T.37. 327.

T.38. 241, 286, 457, 467, 506, 528.

T.39. 474, 481.

The above list of M.T.Bs appears to have been sunk. The remaining numbers
(of which there is no record), were surrendered & scrapped 1946-48.

MOTOR TORPEDO BOAT. (Continued).
T.14. Type. (47 Boats completed).

Displacement. 14.5 Tonnes.   Compliment: 7.
Dimensions: 49'2" x 12'0" x 2'0",
Machinery: Various, 920Bhp = 33.0Kts.
Fuel Cap: Unknown.
Armament: 2 x 18" Torpedo's, 1 x 25.0mmAA or 1 x 13.2mmAA.

Number.	Builder.	Laid dwn.	Launched.	Completed.
TB.549.	Unknown.	Unknown.	1944-45.	Unknown.

Fate: Sunk. Warloss. Cause & Date unknown.

Number.	Builder.	Laid dwn.	Launched.	Completed.
TB.869.	Unknown.	Unknown.	1944-44.	Unknown.

Fate: Sunk. Warloss. Cause & Date unknown.

Number.	Builder.	Laid dwn.	Launched.	Completed.
TB.877.	Unknown.	Unknown.	1944-45.	Unknown.

Fate: Sunk. Warloss. Cause & Date unknown.

Number.	Builder.	Laid dwn.	Launched.	Completed.
TB.883.	Unknown.	Unknown.	1944-45.	Unknown.

Fate: Sunk. Warloss. Cause & Date unknown.

Number.	Builder.	Laid dwn.	Launched.	Completed.
TB.538.	Unknown.	Unknown.	1944-45.	Unknown.

Fate: BU. Post war.

Number.	Builder.	Laid dwn.	Launched.	Completed.
TB.548.	Unknown.	Unknown.	1944-45.	Unknown.

Fate: BU. Post war.

Number.	Builder.	Laid dwn.	Launched.	Completed.
TB.550.	Unknown.	Unknown.	1944-45.	Unknown.

Fate: BU. Post war.

Number.	Builder.	Laid dwn.	Launched.	Completed.
TB.555.	Unknown.	Unknown.	1944-45.	Unknown.

Fate: BU. Post war.

Number.	Builder.	Laid dwn.	Launched.	Completed.
TB.839.	Unknown.	Unknown.	1944-45.	Unknown.

Fate: BU. Post war.

Number.	Builder.	Laid dwn.	Launched.	Completed.
TB.848.	Unknown.	Unknown.	1944-45.	Unknown.

Fate: BU. Post war.

Number.	Builder.	Laid dwn.	Launched.	Completed.
TB.878.	Unknown.	Unknown.	1944-45.	Unknown.

Fate: BU. Post war.

MOTOR TORPEDO BOAT. (Continued).
T.14. Type. (Continued).

Number.	Builder.	Laid dwn.	Launched.	Completed.
TB.882.	Unknown.	Unknown.	1944-45.	Unknown.

Fate: BU. Post war.

T.15. Type.

Displacement.	15.0 Tonnes.		Compliment: 7.
Dimensions:	49'2" x 12'0" x 2'0".		
Machinery:	Various, 920Bhp = 33.0Kts.		
Fuel Cap:	Unknown.		
Armament:	2 x 18" Torpedo's, 1 x 25.0mmAA or 1 x 13.2mmAA.		

Number.	Builder.	Laid dwn.	Launched.	Completed.
TB.1013.	Unknown.	Unknown.	1944-45.	Unknown.

Fate: Sunk. War loss. Cause & Date unknown.

Number.	Builder.	Laid dwn.	Launched.	Completed.
TB.1001.	Unknown.	Unknown.	1944-45.	Unknown.

Fate: BU. Post war.

Number.	Builder.	Laid dwn.	Launched.	Completed.
TB.1008.	Unknown.	Unknown.	1944-45.	Unknown.

Fate: BU. Post war.

Number.	Builder.	Laid dwn.	Launched.	Completed.
TB.1011.	Unknown.	Unknown.	1944-45.	Unknown.

Fate: BU. Post war.

Number.	Builder.	Laid dwn.	Launched.	Completed.
TB.1012.	Unknown.	Unknown.	1944-45.	Unknown.

Fate: BU. Post war.

Number.	Builder.	Laid dwn.	Launched.	Completed.
TB.1014.	Unknown.	Unknown.	1944-45.	Unknown.

Fate: BU. Post war.

Number.	Builder.	Laid dwn.	Launched.	Completed.
TB.1031.	Unknown.	Unknown.	1944-45.	Unknown.

Fate: BU. Post war.

MOTOR TORPEDO BOAT. (Continued).
T.51. Type. (8 Boats completed).

Displacement. 84.2 Tonnes.   Compliment: 18.
Dimensions: 106'3" x 16'5" x 3'8".
Machinery: Various, 3600Bhp = 29.0Kts.
Fuel Cap: Unknown.
Armament: 2 x 18" Torpedo's, 3 x 25.0mmAA, 8 x DCs.

Number.	Builder.	Laid dwn.	Launched.	Completed.
TB.10.	Unknown.	Unknown.	1942-45.	Unknown.

Fate: Sunk. War loss. Cause & Date unknown.

Number.	Builder.	Laid dwn.	Launched.	Completed.
TB.11.	Unknown.	Unknown.	1942-45.	Unknown.

Fate: BU. Post war.

Number.	Builder.	Laid dwn.	Launched.	Completed.
TB.12.	Unknown.	Unknown.	1942-45.	Unknown.

Fate: Sunk. War loss. Cause & Date unknown.

Number.	Builder.	Laid dwn.	Launched.	Completed.
TB.13.	Unknown.	Unknown.	1942-45.	Unknown.

Fate: BU. Post war.

Number.	Builder.	Laid dwn.	Launched.	Completed.
TB.14.	Unknown.	Unknown.	1942-45.	Unknown.

Fate: Constructional loss. Cause & Date unknown.

Number.	Builder.	Laid dwn.	Launched.	Completed.
TB.15.	Unknown.	Unknown.	1942-45.	Unknown.

Fate: Constructional loss. Cause & Date unknown.

Number.	Builder.	Laid dwn.	Launched.	Completed.
TB.16.	Unknown.	Unknown.	1942-45.	Unknown.

Fate: Constructional loss. Cause & Date unknown.

Number.	Builder.	Laid dwn.	Launched.	Completed.
TB.17.	Unknown.	Unknown.	1942-45.	Unknown.

Fate: BU. Post war.

MOTOR GUN BOAT.
H.1. Type. (1 only built).

Displacement. 26.2 Tonnes.   Compliment: 18.
Dimensions: 59'1" x 14'9" x 2'8".
Machinery: Various, 1840Bhp = 33.0Kts.
Fuel Cap: Unknown.
Armament: 2 x 20mmAA, 2 x 7.7mmAA, 2 x DCs.

Number.	Builder.	Laid dwn.	Launched.	Completed.
TB.01.	Unknown.	Unknown.	1942-45.	Unknown.

Fate: Sunk. War loss. Cause & Date unknown.

H.2. Type. (7 only built).

Displacement. 25.0 Tonnes.   Compliment: 18.
Dimensions: 59'1" x 14'1" x 2'5".
Machinery: Various, 1840Bhp = 34.0Kts.
Fuel Cap: Unknown.
Armament: 2 x 18.0" Torpedoes, 3 x 25.0mmAA, 4 x DCs.
                Alt. 1 x 25.0mmAA, or 1 x 13.2mmAA.

Number.	Builder.	Laid dwn.	Launched.	Completed.
TB.02.	Unknown.	Unknown.	1942-45.	Unknown.

Fate: BU. Post war.

Number.	Builder.	Laid dwn.	Launched.	Completed.
TB.03.	Unknown.	Unknown.	1942-45.	Unknown.

Fate: Sunk. War loss. Cause & Date unknown.

Number.	Builder.	Laid dwn.	Launched.	Completed.
TB.04.	Unknown.	Unknown.	1942-45.	Unknown.

Fate: Sunk. War loss. Cause & Date unknown.

Number.	Builder.	Laid dwn.	Launched.	Completed.
TB.05.	Unknown.	Unknown.	1942-45.	Unknown.

Fate: Sunk. War loss. Cause & Date unknown.

Number.	Builder.	Laid dwn.	Launched.	Completed.
TB.06.	Unknown.	Unknown.	1942-45.	Unknown.

Fate: BU. Post war.

Number.	Builder.	Laid dwn.	Launched.	Completed.
TB.07.	Unknown.	Unknown.	1942-45.	Unknown.

Fate: Sunk. War loss. Cause & Date unknown.

Number.	Builder.	Laid dwn.	Launched.	Completed.
TB.08.	Unknown.	Unknown.	1942-45.	Unknown.

Fate: Sunk. War loss. Cause & Date unknown.

MOTOR GUN BOAT.

H.35. Type.

Displacement, 25.0 Tonnes.   Compliment: 7.
Dimensions: 59'1" x 14'1" x 2'5".
Machinery: Various, 1840Bhp = 34.0Kts.
Fuel Cap: Unknown.
Armament: 2 x 18.0" Torpedoes, 3 x 25.0mmAA, 4 x DCs.
                Alt. 1 x 25.0mmAA, or 1 x 13.2mmAA.

Number.	Builder.	Laid dwn.	Launched.	Completed.
TB.27.	Unknown.	Unknown.	1943-44.	Unknown.

Fate: BU. Post war.

Number.	Builder.	Laid dwn.	Launched.	Completed.
TB.28.	Unknown.	Unknown.	1943-44.	Unknown.

Fate: Sunk. War loss. Cause & Date unknown.

Number.	Builder.	Laid dwn.	Launched.	Completed.
TB.29.	Unknown.	Unknown.	1943-44.	Unknown.

Fate: BU. Post war.

Number.	Builder.	Laid dwn.	Launched.	Completed.
TB.30.	Unknown.	Unknown.	1943-44.	Unknown.

Fate: BU. Post war.

Number.	Builder.	Laid dwn.	Launched.	Completed.
TB.31.	Unknown.	Unknown.	1943-44.	Unknown.

Fate: BU. Post war.

Number.	Builder.	Laid dwn.	Launched.	Completed.
TB.32.	Unknown.	Unknown.	1943-44.	Unknown.

Fate: BU. Post war.

Number.	Builder.	Laid dwn.	Launched.	Completed.
TB.201.	Unknown.	Unknown.	1943-44.	Unknown.

Fate: BU. Post war.

Number.	Builder.	Laid dwn.	Launched.	Completed.
TB.202.	Unknown.	Unknown.	1943-44.	Unknown.

Fate: BU. Post war.

Number.	Builder.	Laid dwn.	Launched.	Completed.
TB.203.	Unknown.	Unknown.	1943-44.	Unknown.

Fate: BU. Post war.

Number.	Builder.	Laid dwn.	Launched.	Completed.
TB.204.	Unknown.	Unknown.	1943-44.	Unknown.

Fate: BU. Post war.

MOTOR GUN BOAT. (Continued).

H.35. Type. (Continued).

Number.	Builder.	Laid dwn.	Launched.	Completed.
TB.206.	Unknown.	Unknown.	1943-44.	Unknown.

Fate: BU. Post war.

Number.	Builder.	Laid dwn.	Launched.	Completed.
TB.207.	Unknown.	Unknown.	1943-44.	Unknown.

Fate: BU. Post war.

H.38. Type.

Displacement. 24.8 Tonnes.	Compliment: 7.

Dimensions: 59'1" x 14'1" x 2'5".
Machinery: Various, 1400Bhp = 27.0Kts.
Fuel Cap: Unknown.
Armament: 2 x 18.0" Torpedoes, 3 x 25.0mmAA, 4 x DCs.
Alt. 1 x 25.0mmAA, or 1 x 13.2mmAA.

Number.	Builder.	Laid dwn.	Launched.	Completed.
TB.11.	Unknown.	Unknown.	1943-44.	Unknown.

Fate: Sunk. War loss. Cause & Date unknown.

Number.	Builder.	Laid dwn.	Launched.	Completed.
TB.12.	Unknown.	Unknown.	1943-44.	Unknown.

Fate: BU. Post war.

Number.	Builder.	Laid dwn.	Launched.	Completed.
TB.13.	Unknown.	Unknown.	1943-44.	Unknown.

Fate: BU. Post war.

Number.	Builder.	Laid dwn.	Launched.	Completed.
TB.14.	Unknown.	Unknown.	1943-44.	Unknown.

Fate: BU. Post war.

Number.	Builder.	Laid dwn.	Launched.	Completed.
TB.15.	Unknown.	Unknown.	1943-44.	Unknown.

Fate: BU. Post war.

Number.	Builder.	Laid dwn.	Launched.	Completed.
TB.16.	Unknown.	Unknown.	1943-44.	Unknown.

Fate: BU. Post war.

Number.	Builder.	Laid dwn.	Launched.	Completed.
TB.17.	Unknown.	Unknown.	1943-44.	Unknown.

Fate: BU. Post war.

Number.	Builder.	Laid dwn.	Launched.	Completed.
TB.18.	Unknown.	Unknown.	1943-44.	Unknown.

Fate: BU. Post war.

MOTOR GUN BOAT. (Continued).

H.38. Type. (Continued).

Number.	Builder.	Laid dwn.	Launched.	Completed.
TB.19.	Unknown.	Unknown.	1943-44.	Unknown.

Fate: Sunk. War loss. Cause & Date unknown.

Number.	Builder.	Laid dwn.	Launched.	Completed.
TB.20.	Unknown.	Unknown.	1943-44.	Unknown.

Fate: Sunk. War loss. Cause & Date unknown.

Number.	Builder.	Laid dwn.	Launched.	Completed.
TB.21.	Unknown.	Unknown.	1943-44.	Unknown.

Fate: BU. Post war.

Number.	Builder.	Laid dwn.	Launched.	Completed.
TB.22.	Unknown.	Unknown.	1943-44.	Unknown.

Fate: BU. Post war.

Number.	Builder.	Laid dwn.	Launched.	Completed.
TB.23.	Unknown.	Unknown.	1943-44.	Unknown.

Fate: BU. Post war.

Number.	Builder.	Laid dwn.	Launched.	Completed.
TB.24.	Unknown.	Unknown.	1943-44.	Unknown.

Fate: BU. Post war.

Number.	Builder.	Laid dwn.	Launched.	Completed.
TB.25.	Unknown.	Unknown.	1943-44.	Unknown.

Fate: Sunk. War loss. Cause & Date unknown.

Number.	Builder.	Laid dwn.	Launched.	Completed.
TB.26.	Unknown.	Unknown.	1943-44.	Unknown.

Fate: BU. Post war.

TB.27. to TB.50. No records available.

Number.	Builder.	Laid dwn.	Launched.	Completed.
TB.51.	Unknown.	Unknown.	1943-44.	Unknown.

Fate: BU. Post war.

Number.	Builder.	Laid dwn.	Launched.	Completed.
TB.52.	Unknown.	Unknown.	1943-44.	Unknown.

Fate: BU. Post war.

Number.	Builder.	Laid dwn.	Launched.	Completed.
TB.53.	Unknown.	Unknown.	1943-44.	Unknown.

Fate: BU. Post war.

Number.	Builder.	Laid dwn.	Launched.	Completed.
TB.54.	Unknown.	Unknown.	1943-44.	Unknown.

Fate: BU. Post war.

MOTOR GUN BOAT. (Continued).

H.38. Type. (Continued).

Number.	Builder.	Laid dwn.	Launched.	Completed.
TB.55.	Unknown.	Unknown.	1943-44.	Unknown.

Fate: Sunk. War loss. Cause & Date unknown.

Number.	Builder.	Laid dwn.	Launched.	Completed.
TB.56.	Unknown.	Unknown.	1943-44.	Unknown.

Fate: BU. Post war.

Number.	Builder.	Laid dwn.	Launched.	Completed.
TB.57.	Unknown.	Unknown.	1943-44.	Unknown.

Fate: BU. Post war.

Number.	Builder.	Laid dwn.	Launched.	Completed.
TB.58.	Unknown.	Unknown.	1943-44.	Unknown.

Fate: BU. Post war.

Number.	Builder.	Laid dwn.	Launched.	Completed.
TB.59.	Unknown.	Unknown.	1943-44.	Unknown.

Fate: BU. Post war.

Number.	Builder.	Laid dwn.	Launched.	Completed.
TB.60.	Unknown.	Unknown.	1943-44.	Unknown.

Fate: BU. Post war.

Number.	Builder.	Laid dwn.	Launched.	Completed.
TB.61.	Unknown.	Unknown.	1943-44.	Unknown.

Fate: Sunk. War loss. Cause & Date unknown.

Number.	Builder.	Laid dwn.	Launched.	Completed.
TB.62.	Unknown.	Unknown.	1943-44.	Unknown.

Fate: Sunk. War loss. Cause & Date unknown.

Number.	Builder.	Laid dwn.	Launched.	Completed.
TB.63.	Unknown.	Unknown.	1943-44.	Unknown.

Fate: BU. Post war.

Number.	Builder.	Laid dwn.	Launched.	Completed.
TB.64.	Unknown.	Unknown.	1943-44.	Unknown.

Fate: BU. Post war.

Number.	Builder.	Laid dwn.	Launched.	Completed.
TB.65.	Unknown.	Unknown.	1943-44.	Unknown.

Fate: BU. Post war.

Number.	Builder.	Laid dwn.	Launched.	Completed.
TB.66.	Unknown.	Unknown.	1943-44.	Unknown.

Fate: BU. Post war.

MOTOR GUN BOAT. (Continued).

H.38. Type. (Continued).

Number.	Builder.	Laid dwn.	Launched.	Completed.
TB.67.	Unknown.	Unknown.	1943-44.	Unknown.

Fate: Sunk. War loss. Cause & Date unknown.

Number.	Builder.	Laid dwn.	Launched.	Completed.
TB.68.	Unknown.	Unknown.	1943-44.	Unknown.

Fate: BU. Post war.

Number.	Builder.	Laid dwn.	Launched.	Completed.
TB.69.	Unknown.	Unknown.	1943-44.	Unknown.

Fate: BU. Post war.

Number.	Builder.	Laid dwn.	Launched.	Completed.
TB.70.	Unknown.	Unknown.	1943-44.	Unknown.

Fate: BU. Post war.

Number.	Builder.	Laid dwn.	Launched.	Completed.
TB.71.	Unknown.	Unknown.	1943-44.	Unknown.

Fate: BU. Post war.

Number.	Builder.	Laid dwn.	Launched.	Completed.
TB.72.	Unknown.	Unknown.	1943-44.	Unknown.

Fate: BU. Post war.

Number.	Builder.	Laid dwn.	Launched.	Completed.
TB.73.	Unknown.	Unknown.	1943-44.	Unknown.

Fate: BU. Post war.

Number.	Builder.	Laid dwn.	Launched.	Completed.
TB.74.	Unknown.	Unknown.	1943-44.	Unknown.

Fate: BU. Post war.

Number.	Builder.	Laid dwn.	Launched.	Completed.
TB.75.	Unknown.	Unknown.	1943-44.	Unknown.

Fate: BU. Post war.

Number.	Builder.	Laid dwn.	Launched.	Completed.
TB.76.	Unknown.	Unknown.	1943-44.	Unknown.

Fate: BU. Post war.

Number.	Builder.	Laid dwn.	Launched.	Completed.
TB.77.	Unknown.	Unknown.	1943-44.	Unknown.

Fate: BU. Post war.

Number.	Builder.	Laid dwn.	Launched.	Completed.
TB.78.	Unknown.	Unknown.	1943-44.	Unknown.

Fate: BU. Post war.

MOTOR GUN BOAT. (Continued).

H.38. Type. (Continued).

Number.	Builder.	Laid dwn.	Launched.	Completed.
TB.79.	Unknown.	Unknown.	1943-44.	Unknown.

Fate: BU. Post war.

Number.	Builder.	Laid dwn.	Launched.	Completed.
TB.81.	Unknown.	Unknown.	1943-44.	Unknown.

Fate: BU. Post war.

Number.	Builder.	Laid dwn.	Launched.	Completed.
TB.82.	Unknown.	Unknown.	1943-44.	Unknown.

Fate: BU. Post war.

Number.	Builder.	Laid dwn.	Launched.	Completed.
TB.83.	Unknown.	Unknown.	1943-44.	Unknown.

Fate: BU. Post war.

Number.	Builder.	Laid dwn.	Launched.	Completed.
TB.84.	Unknown.	Unknown.	1943-44.	Unknown.

Fate: BU. Post war.

Number.	Builder.	Laid dwn.	Launched.	Completed.
TB.85.	Unknown.	Unknown.	1943-44.	Unknown.

Fate: BU. Post war.

Number.	Builder.	Laid dwn.	Launched.	Completed.
TB.86.	Unknown.	Unknown.	1943-44.	Unknown.

Fate: BU. Post war.

Number.	Builder.	Laid dwn.	Launched.	Completed.
TB.87.	Unknown.	Unknown.	1943-44.	Unknown.

Fate: BU. Post war.

Number.	Builder.	Laid dwn.	Launched.	Completed.
TB.88.	Unknown.	Unknown.	1943-44.	Unknown.

Fate: BU. Post war.

Number.	Builder.	Laid dwn.	Launched.	Completed.
TB.89.	Unknown.	Unknown.	1943-44.	Unknown.

Fate: BU. Post war.

Number.	Builder.	Laid dwn.	Launched.	Completed.
TB.90.	Unknown.	Unknown.	1943-44.	Unknown.

Fate: BU. Post war.

Number.	Builder.	Laid dwn.	Launched.	Completed.
TB.91.	Unknown.	Unknown.	1943-44.	Unknown.

Fate: BU. Post war.

MOTOR GUN BOAT. (Continued).

H.38. Type. (Continued).

Number.	Builder.	Laid dwn.	Launched.	Completed.
TB.92.	Unknown.	Unknown.	1943–44.	Unknown.

Fate: BU. Post war.

Number.	Builder.	Laid dwn.	Launched.	Completed.
TB.93.	Unknown.	Unknown.	1943–44.	Unknown.

Fate: BU. Post war.

Number.	Builder.	Laid dwn.	Launched.	Completed.
TB.94.	Unknown.	Unknown.	1943–44.	Unknown.

Fate: BU. Post war.

Number.	Builder.	Laid dwn.	Launched.	Completed.
TB.95.	Unknown.	Unknown.	1943–44.	Unknown.

Fate: BU. Post war.

Number.	Builder.	Laid dwn.	Launched.	Completed.
TB.96.	Unknown.	Unknown.	1943–44.	Unknown.

Fate: BU. Post war.

Number.	Builder.	Laid dwn.	Launched.	Completed.
TB.97.	Unknown.	Unknown.	1943–44.	Unknown.

Fate: BU. Post war.

Number.	Builder.	Laid dwn.	Launched.	Completed.
TB.98.	Unknown.	Unknown.	1943–44.	Unknown.

Fate: BU. Post war.

Number.	Builder.	Laid dwn.	Launched.	Completed.
TB.99.	Unknown.	Unknown.	1943–44.	Unknown.

Fate: BU. Post war.

Number.	Builder.	Laid dwn.	Launched.	Completed.
TB.100.	Unknown.	Unknown.	1943–44.	Unknown.

Fate: BU. Post war.

MOTOR GUN BOAT. (Continued).

H.61. Type.

Displacement. 25.6 Tonnes.		Compliment: 7.
Dimensions:	62'4" x 14'4" x 2'5".	
Machinery:	Various, 600Bhp = 17.5Kts.	
Fuel Cap:	Unknown.	
Armament:	3 x 25.0mmAA, 3 x DCs.	

Number.	Builder.	Laid dwn.	Launched.	Completed.
TB.33.	Unknown.	Unknown.	1944-45.	Unknown.

Fate: Sunk. Cause & Date unknown.

Number.	Builder.	Laid dwn.	Launched.	Completed.
TB.34.	Unknown.	Unknown.	1944-45.	Unknown.

Fate: Sunk. Cause & Date Unknown.

Number.	Builder.	Laid dwn.	Launched.	Completed.
TB.35.	Unknown.	Unknown.	1944-45.	Unknown.

Fate: Sunk. Cause & Date unknown.

Number.	Builder.	Laid dwn.	Launched.	Completed.
TB.36.	Unknown.	Unknown.	1944-45.	Unknown.

Fate: Sunk. Cause & Date Unknown.

Number.	Builder.	Laid dwn.	Launched.	Completed.
TB.37.	Unknown.	Unknown.	1944-45.	Unknown.

Fate: BU. Post war.

Number.	Builder.	Laid dwn.	Launched.	Completed.
TB.38.	Unknown.	Unknown.	1944-45.	Unknown.

Fate: BU. Post war.

Number.	Builder.	Laid dwn.	Launched.	Completed.
TB.39.	Unknown.	Unknown.	1944-45.	Unknown.

Fate: BU. Post war.

Number.	Builder.	Laid dwn.	Launched.	Completed.
TB.40.	Unknown.	Unknown.	1944-45.	Unknown.

Fate: BU. Post war.

Number.	Builder.	Laid dwn.	Launched.	Completed.
TB.41.	Unknown.	Unknown.	1944-45.	Unknown.

Fate: Sunk. Cause & Date Unknown.

Number.	Builder.	Laid dwn.	Launched.	Completed.
TB.42.	Unknown.	Unknown.	1944-45.	Unknown.

Fate: BU. Post war.

MOTOR GUN BOAT. (Continued).

H.61. Type. (Continued).

Number	Builder	Laid dwn.	Launched.	Completed.
TB.43.	Unknown.	Unknown.	1944-45.	Unknown.

Fate: BU. Post war.

Number.	Builder.	Laid dwn.	Launched.	Completed.
TB.44.	Unknown.	Unknown.	1944-45.	Unknown.

Fate: BU. Post war.

Number.	Builder.	Laid dwn.	Launched.	Completed.
TB.45.	Unknown.	Unknown.	1944-45.	Unknown.

Fate: BU. Post war.

Number.	Builder.	Laid dwn.	Launched.	Completed.
TB.46.	Unknown.	Unknown.	1944-45.	Unknown.

Fate: Sunk. Cause & Date Unknown.

TB.47 to TB.100 No INFO.

Number.	Builder.	Laid dwn.	Launched.	Completed.
TB.101.	Unknown.	Unknown.	1944-45.	Unknown.

Fate: BU. Post war.

Number.	Builder.	Laid dwn.	Launched.	Completed.
TB.102.	Unknown.	Unknown.	1944-45.	Unknown.

Fate: Sunk. Cause & Date Unknown.

Number.	Builder.	Laid dwn.	Launched.	Completed.
TB.103.	Unknown.	Unknown.	1944-45.	Unknown.

Fate: BU. Post war.

Number.	Builder.	Laid dwn.	Launched.	Completed.
TB104.	Unknown.	Unknown.	1944-45.	Unknown.

Fate: BU. Post war.

Number.	Builder.	Laid dwn.	Launched.	Completed.
TB.105.	Unknown.	Unknown.	1944-45.	Unknown.

Fate: BU. Post war.

Number.	Builder.	Laid dwn.	Launched.	Completed.
TB.106.	Unknown.	Unknown.	1944-45.	Unknown.

Fate: Sunk. Cause & Date Unknown.

Number.	Builder.	Laid dwn.	Launched.	Completed.
TB.107.	Unknown.	Unknown.	1944-45.	Unknown.

Fate: BU. Post war.

MOTOR GUN BOAT. (Continued).

H.61. Type. (Continued).

Number.	Builder.	Laid dwn.	Launched.	Completed.
TB108.	Unknown.	Unknown.	1944-45.	Unknown.

Fate: BU. Post war.

Number.	Builder.	Laid dwn.	Launched.	Completed.
TB.109.	Unknown.	Unknown.	1944-45.	Unknown.

Fate: BU. Post war.

Number.	Builder.	Laid dwn.	Launched.	Completed.
TB.110.	Unknown.	Unknown.	1944-45.	Unknown.

Fate: BU. Post war.

Number.	Builder.	Laid dwn.	Launched.	Completed.
TB111.	Unknown.	Unknown.	1944-45.	Unknown.

Fate: BU. Post war.

Number.	Builder.	Laid dwn.	Launched.	Completed.
TB.112.	Unknown.	Unknown.	1944-45.	Unknown.

Fate: BU. Post war.

Number.	Builder.	Laid dwn.	Launched.	Completed.
TB.113.	Unknown.	Unknown.	1944-45.	Unknown.

Fate: Sunk. Cause & Date Unknown.

Number.	Builder.	Laid dwn.	Launched.	Completed.
TB.114.	Unknown.	Unknown.	1944-45.	Unknown.

Fate: BU. Post war.

Number.	Builder.	Laid dwn.	Launched.	Completed.
TB115.	Unknown.	Unknown.	1944-45.	Unknown.

Fate: BU. Post war.

Number.	Builder.	Laid dwn.	Launched.	Completed.
TB.116.	Unknown.	Unknown.	1944-45.	Unknown.

Fate: BU. Post war.

Number.	Builder.	Laid dwn.	Launched.	Completed.
TB.117.	Unknown.	Unknown.	1944-45.	Unknown.

Fate: BU. Post war.

Number.	Builder.	Laid dwn.	Launched.	Completed.
TB118.	Unknown.	Unknown.	1944-45.	Unknown.

Fate: BU. Post war.

Number.	Builder.	Laid dwn.	Launched.	Completed.
TB.119.	Unknown.	Unknown.	1944-45.	Unknown.

Fate: BU. Post war.

MOTOR GUN BOAT. (Continued).

H.61. Type. (Continued).

Number.	Builder.	Laid dwn.	Launched.	Completed.
TB.120.	Unknown.	Unknown.	1944-45.	Unknown.

Fate: BU. Post war.

Number.	Builder.	Laid dwn.	Launched.	Completed.
TB121.	Unknown.	Unknown.	1944-45.	Unknown.

Fate: BU. Post war.

Number .	Builder.	Laid dwn.	Launched.	Completed.
TB.122.	Unknown.	Unknown.	1944-45.	Unknown.

Fate: BU. Post war.

Number.	Builder.	Laid dwn.	Launched.	Completed.
TB.123.	Unknown.	Unknown.	1944-45.	Unknown.

Fate: BU. Post war.

Number.	Builder.	Laid dwn.	Launched.	Completed.
TB124.	Unknown.	Unknown.	1944-45.	Unknown.

Fate: BU. Post war.

TB.125. to TB.221. No Info.

Number.	Builder.	Laid dwn.	Launched.	Completed.
TB.222.	Unknown.	Unknown.	1944-45.	Unknown.

Fate: Sunk. Cause & Date Unknown.

Number.	Builder.	Laid dwn.	Launched.	Completed.
TB.223.	Unknown.	Unknown.	1944-45.	Unknown.

Fate: Sunk. Cause & Date Unknown.

Number.	Builder.	Laid dwn.	Launched.	Completed.
TB.224.	Unknown.	Unknown.	1944-45.	Unknown.

Fate: BU. Post war.

Number.	Builder.	Laid dwn.	Launched.	Completed.
TB.225.	Unknown.	Unknown.	1944-45.	Unknown.

Fate: BU. Post war.

Number.	Builder.	Laid dwn.	Launched.	Completed.
TB.226.	Unknown.	Unknown.	1944-45.	Unknown.

Fate: BU. Post war.

Number.	Builder.	Laid dwn.	Launched.	Completed.
TB.227.	Unknown.	Unknown.	1944-45.	Unknown.

Fate: BU. Post war.

MOTOR GUN BOAT. (Continued).

H.61. Type. (Continued).

Number.	Builder.	Laid dwn.	Launched.	Completed.
TB.228.	Unknown.	Unknown.	1944-45.	Unknown.

Fate: BU. Post war.

Number.	Builder.	Laid dwn.	Launched.	Completed.
TB.229.	Unknown.	Unknown.	1944-45.	Unknown.

Fate: BU. Post war.

Number.	Builder.	Laid dwn.	Launched.	Completed.
TB.230.	Unknown.	Unknown.	1944-45.	Unknown.

Fate: BU. Post war.

Number.	Builder.	Laid dwn.	Launched.	Completed.
TB.231.	Unknown.	Unknown.	1944-45.	Unknown.

Fate: BU. Post war.

Number.	Builder.	Laid dwn.	Launched.	Completed.
TB.232.	Unknown.	Unknown.	1944-45.	Unknown.

Fate: BU. Post war.

Number.	Builder.	Laid dwn.	Launched.	Completed.
TB.233.	Unknown.	Unknown.	1944-45.	Unknown.

Fate: BU. Post war.

Number.	Builder.	Laid dwn.	Launched.	Completed.
TB.234.	Unknown.	Unknown.	1944-45.	Unknown.

Fate: BU. Post war.

Number.	Builder.	Laid dwn.	Launched.	Completed.
TB.235.	Unknown.	Unknown.	1944-45.	Unknown.

Fate: BU. Post war.

Number.	Builder.	Laid dwn.	Launched.	Completed.
TB.236.	Unknown.	Unknown.	1944-45.	Unknown.

Fate: BU. Post war.

Number.	Builder.	Laid dwn.	Launched.	Completed.
TB.237.	Unknown.	Unknown.	1944-45.	Unknown.

Fate: BU. Post war.

Number.	Builder.	Laid dwn.	Launched.	Completed.
TB.238.	Unknown.	Unknown.	1944-45.	Unknown.

Fate: BU. Post war.

Number.	Builder.	Laid dwn.	Launched.	Completed.
TB.239.	Unknown.	Unknown.	1944-45.	Unknown.

Fate: BU. Post war.

MOTOR GUN BOAT. (Continued).

H.61. Type. (Continued).

Number	Builder	Laid dwn.	Launched.	Completed.
TB.240.	Unknown.	Unknown.	1944-45.	Unknown.

Fate: BU. Post war.

Number.	Builder.	Laid dwn.	Launched.	Completed.
TB.241.	Unknown.	Unknown.	1944-45.	Unknown.

Fate: BU. Post war.

Number.	Builder.	Laid dwn.	Launched.	Completed.
TB.242.	Unknown.	Unknown.	1944-45.	Unknown.

Fate: BU. Post war.

Number.	Builder.	Laid dwn.	Launched.	Completed.
TB.243.	Unknown.	Unknown.	1944-45.	Unknown.

Fate: BU. Post war.

Number.	Builder.	Laid dwn.	Launched.	Completed.
TB.244.	Unknown.	Unknown.	1944-45.	Unknown.

Fate: BU. Post war.

Number.	Builder.	Laid dwn.	Launched.	Completed.
TB.245.	Unknown.	Unknown.	1944-45.	Unknown.

Fate: BU. Post war.

MOTOR LAUNCHES.

15.M. TYPE. (Approximately 40 Built).

Displacement. 10.0 Tonnes.　　　　**Compliment:** 7.
Dimensions: 49'2" x 10'10" x 1'11".
Machinery: Various, 120Bhp = 11.0Kts.
Fuel Cap: Unknown.
Armament: 3 x 25.0mmAA, or 1 x 7.7mmAA.
No further details available.

MOTOR LAUNCHES.

19.M. TYPE. (Approximately 48 Built).

Displacement. 25.6 Tonnes.　　　　**Compliment:** 7.
Dimensions: 62'4" x 14'4" x 2'5".
Machinery: Various, 600Bhp = 17.5Kts.
Fuel Cap: Unknown.
Armament: 3 x 25.0mmAA, or1 x 7.7mmAA.
No further details available.

MOTOR LAUNCHES.

25.T. TYPE. (Approximately 80 Built).

Displacement. 26.0 Tonnes.　　　　**Compliment:** Unknown.
Dimensions: 59'0" x 11'6" x 2'4".
Machinery: Various, 300Bhp = 11.0Kts.
Fuel Cap: Unknown.
Armament: 2 x 13.2mmAA.
No further details available.

SUICIDE CRAFT.

SHINYO TYPE. (Approximately 6000 Built).

Displacement. 2.15 Tonnes.　　　　**Compliment:** 1 or 2.
Dimensions: 16'9" x 5'6" x 1'1".
Machinery: Various, 134Bhp = 20-28Kts.
Fuel Cap: Unknown.
Armament: 1 x 13.2mmAA, 2 x 4.7" Rockets.
Extremely limited success.
No further details available.

MIDGET SUBMARINES.

A. Type. Built-1934-42.

Displacement 45.3 Tonnes Submerged. Compliment: 1 or 2.
Dimensions: 78'5" x 6'1" x 6'1".
Machinery: 1 shaft Electric motor, 600hp = 19-24Kts.
Endurance: (Submerged) 17 Nm @ 19Kts or 80 Nm @ 2Kts.
Fuel Cap: Unknown.
Armament: 2 x 18" Torpedoes.
No further details available.

MIDGET SUBMARINES.

B & C. Type. Built-1943-44.

Displacement. 49.0 Tonnes Submerged.   Compliment: 3.
Dimensions: 81'8" x 6'2" x 6'2".
Machinery: 1 shaft Diesel/Elect motor, 600Bhp=18.5Kts, 40Bhp=6.5Kts.
Fuel Cap: Unknown.
Armament: 2 x 18" Torpedoes.
No further details available.

MIDGET SUBMARINES.

D. Type. (KORYU) Built-1944-45. (Approximately 115 Built).

Displacement. 58.4 Tonnes Submerged.   Compliment: 5.
Dimensions: 86'1" x 6'8" x 6'7".
Machinery: 1 shaft Diesel/Elect motor, 500Bhp=16.0Kts, 150Bhp=8.0Kts.
Endurance: Surface-1000Nm @ 8Kts. Submerged-125Nm @ 2.5Kts.
Fuel Cap: Unknown.
Armament: 2 x 18" Torpedoes.
No further details available.

MIDGET SUBMARINES.

KAIRYU. Type. Built-1945. (Approximately 212 Built).

Displacement. 18.97 Tonnes Submerged. Compliment: 2.
Dimensions: 56'8" x 4'3" x 4'3".
Machinery: 1 shaft Diesel/Elect motor,85Bhp=10.0Kts, 80Bhp=7.5Kts.
Endurance: Surface-450Nm @ 5Kts. Submerged-36Nm @ 3.0Kts.
Fuel Cap: Unknown.
Armament: 2 x 18" Torpedoes.
No further details available.

HUMAN TORPEDOES.

KAITEN. Type 1. Built-1944-45. (Approximately 400 Built).

Displacement. 18.97 Tonnes Submerged. **Compliment: 2.**
Dimensions: 48'5" x 3'3" x 3'3".
Machinery: Various, 550Bhp = 3.0Kts.
Armament: 3410 Lb Explosive warhead.
No further details available.

HUMAN TORPEDOES.

KAITEN. Type 2 & 4. Built-1945. (Approximately 20 Built).

Displacement. 18.0 Tonnes Submerged. **Compliment: 2.**
Dimensions: 54'1" x 4'5" x 4'5".
Machinery: Liquid Oxygen Engines, 1500Bhp = 40.0Kts.
Armament: 3960 Lb Explosive warhead.
No further details available.

JAPANESE NAVY.
Summing Up.

BATTLESHIPS.	Total 9.	Sunk 7.
AIRCRAFT CARRIERS.	Total 29.	Sunk 20.
CRUISERS.	Total 33.	Sunk 30.
DESTROYERS.	Total 154.	Sunk 115.
TORPEDO BOATS.	Total 12.	Sunk 10.
SUBMARINES.	Total 239.	Sunk 147.
PATROL BOATS.	Total 15.	Sunk 9.
ESCORTS.	Total 166.	Sunk 63.
MINELAYERS.	Total 35.	Sunk 31.
MINESWEEPERS.	Total 35.	Sunk 31.
SUB CHASERS.	Total 29.	Sunk 15.
MISCELLANEOUS.	Total 10.	Sunk 3.
COASTAL ESCORTS.	Total 56.	Sunk 4.
SURVEY SHIP.	Total 1.	Sunk 1.
SEAPLANE CARRIERS.	Total 6.	Sunk 3.
FLYING BOAT TENDER.	Total 1.	Sunk 1.
AIRCRAFT TRANSPORT.	Total 2.	Sunk 1.
LANDING SHIP.	Total 1413.	Sunk 72.
COASTAL FORCES.	Total 6435.	Sunk 80.
MIDGET SUBMARINES.	Unknown.	Unknown.
HUMAN TORPEDOES.	Total 420.	Unknown.